"In *3 Big Questions*, Kara Po through so much of the guesswork and m it so much harder to conne combination of research, p exactly what church leaders

Care

"Kara and Brad help us understand the ... s are confronting today, identify their greatest longings, and g... ..s practical ways to proactively initiate conversations and connections that will ultimately lead them closer to Jesus. If you love and care about teenagers, read this book."

Christine Caine, founder of A21 and Propel Women

"As a parent of two teenagers, I am always looking for resources that will help me better understand my children. As a professor of evangelism, I am also looking for resources that develop our ability to witness to the gospel of Jesus Christ. This work by Kara Powell and Brad Griffin offers a valuable resource that engages the full story of the gospel message to speak to the specific context of the teenager. I am grateful for this resource that will effectively serve the church."

Soong-Chan Rah, Robert Munger Professor of Evangelism at Fuller Theological Seminary and author of *The Next Evangelicalism* and *Prophetic Lament*

"For years I've relied on the research and wisdom of Kara Powell and Brad Griffin. No team has done more to understand the spiritual lives of teens. They deftly unpack the unique dilemmas young people are facing in a time and culture of rapid change and upheaval. They also help us avoid the common, well-intentioned mistakes we often make when trying to guide them. Given Kara's and Brad's track record, none of that surprised me. Here's what did: any adult who reads this book will have their faith strengthened as well. While incredibly relevant for teenagers in this moment, there is eternal truth here that transcends all ages."

Skye Jethani, award-winning author of WithGodDaily.com and cohost of the *Holy Post* podcast

"*3 Big Questions* will help you reengage a generation with a bolder, brighter, and braver version of faith. Kara Powell and Brad Griffin will launch your team into discussions that will forever change the conversations you have with this generation."

Reggie Joiner, founder and CEO of Orange

"As a pastor, I regularly reflect on ways to establish deeper connections with the teenagers who are part of our congregation. As a father of two children, this is always on my heart. This book offers a powerful pathway to make these connections a reality. Kara Powell and Brad Griffin have given us a wonderful gift. Our churches and homes will be profoundly impacted if we begin to intentionally wrestle with the three big questions they present."

Rich Villodas, lead pastor of New Life Fellowship Church, New York City

"Every youth worker and parent wonders if they really know what's happening with the teenagers they care about most. *3 Big Questions* empowers you to understand young people and, more importantly, equips you with countless practical ideas for what to say and do so they experience Jesus more fully. This is exactly what's needed to help parents and leaders win with teenagers!"

Doug Fields, cofounder of DownloadYouthMinistry.com

"One of the keys to reaching the most unreached generation today, Gen Z, is knowing the right questions to ask. Fortunately, my friends Kara and Brad—and the entire Fuller Youth Institute team—have created a resource based upon research that explores the three questions most important to today's teenagers. I invite you to join them on this quest of not only understanding these questions but also exploring how the church can be equipped to answer them in Christ-centered ways. My prayer is that this resource will be an essential tool for both connecting with and reaching Gen Z."

Ed Stetzer, Wheaton College

"Kara and Brad take those of us who care for young people on an insightful journey into the influences that are shaping their world today. Along the way, we learn what Jesus has to say about these life-changing topics, and also how to walk alongside our young friends by listening to the questions they are asking while pointing them to the God who lovingly invites them into his bigger story."

Newt Crenshaw, president of Young Life

"*3 Big Questions* combines the wisdom of years of working with teenagers with fresh insights from listening carefully and critically to them—and a willingness to be challenged both by what young people have to say and by what God is saying to and through them. This is not just another youth ministry book. The questions of teenagers in this book will at times bring you to tears while simultaneously inspiring you to press on and to have better conversations with the beloved young people in your life."

Almeda M. Wright, Yale Divinity School, author of *The Spiritual Lives of Young African Americans*

"Having worked with teenagers for many years as a youth pastor and then taught others to do the same while parenting my own, I hear these three such succinct questions (and answers from Jesus) as balm to my soul. Kara Powell and Brad Griffin offer proven insights into how teenagers can not only take on identity, belonging, and purpose but do so in the safety of the name, embrace, and true calling as people in Christ."

Daniel Harrell, editor in chief, *Christianity Today*

"Kara Powell and Brad Griffin offer wisdom and insight that parents, educators, and ministers will benefit from for years to come, as well as offer practical ideas—that can actually be implemented right away—for helping the teens we love navigate the challenging years of adolescence at one of the most difficult points of human history. This book is a gem, a real gift, and essential reading for those in the trenches of helping teens meet Jesus."

Katie Prejean McGrady, speaker, author, and host of *The Katie McGrady Show* on Sirius XM and *Ave Explores* from Ave Maria Press

"*3 Big Questions* captures the tension of our time. Kara and Brad have revealed the core struggles of young people and their relationship with the church and Christ and have given practical ways to help them live out the gospel. Not only is this a guide to reach young people but, if you are open to it, it will also shape your own journey with Christ. This is a must-read for anyone serious about the kingdom work of discipling the next generation."

Tommy Nixon, CEO of Urban Youth Workers Institute

"This book uncomplicates the most complicated part of my relationship with my teens: helping them figure out WHO THEY ARE. Kara and Brad give us a guide to help teenagers unlock their superpowers. I'm forever grateful."

Carlos Whittaker, author of *Enter Wild*, *Kill the Spider*, and *Moment Maker*

"Kara has long been a thought leader in the next gen space, and FYI has always designed solution-based research to help ministry move forward. Here she and Brad go again, inspiring us through transformational questions that matter."

Sam Collier, lead pastor of Hillsong Atlanta and founder of A Greater Story

"*3 Big Questions* is a very exciting book, because with depth and sensitivity it wades into the most central and mysterious of our human questions. And more importantly, it beckons churches to observe and learn from how young people answer them. But the book does more. It also invites parents, youth workers, pastors, and anyone who cares about young people to see these questions as an invitation into a pilgrimage with them."

Andrew Root, Luther Seminary, author of *The End of Youth Ministry?* and *The Congregation in a Secular Age*

"If you are a parent, youth worker, or church leader who has desired to reach youth, this is a must-read. Our question is usually, How can we reach teenagers? The better question is, How can teenagers reach us? Kara and Brad tell us it starts with listening. This book will inspire you to talk to every young person you come in contact with and give you tools to make you feel like a youth conversationalist."

Gabriel Zamora, pastor, speaker, and CEO of Kingdom Global Ministries

"Kara and Brad's thoughtful, wise, and research-backed book will help those who seek to serve and walk alongside young people not necessarily provide easy answers but help them process their big questions. Packed with practical guidance and opportunities to reflect and apply, it will make you a better listener, provide you with rich insight into the inner lives of real young people, and invite you to draw more impactful connections between the stories of the teenagers in your care and the transformational story of the greatest answer of all."

Martin Saunders, head of innovation at Youthscape, UK, and director of Satellites

"Kara Powell and Brad Griffin are once again paving the road toward better youth discipleship. *3 Big Questions* provides a comprehensive handbook for any context. The stories gathered by the research team create a mosaic that reflects a diverse community. Countless recipes full of tools for adults are grounded in Scripture, are easy to understand, and will give depth to any conversation with teenagers. Destined to be another classic from the Fuller Youth Institute, this is a welcome addition for youth leaders everywhere."

Virginia Ward, Gordon-Conwell Theological Seminary

3 BIG
QUESTIONS
THAT CHANGE EVERY
TEENAGER

3 BIG
QUESTIONS
THAT CHANGE EVERY
TEENAGER

MAKING THE MOST OF YOUR
CONVERSATIONS AND CONNECTIONS

KARA POWELL and
BRAD M. GRIFFIN

BakerBooks
a division of Baker Publishing Group
Grand Rapids, Michigan

© 2021 by Kara E. Powell and Brad M. Griffin

Published by Baker Books
a division of Baker Publishing Group
PO Box 6287, Grand Rapids, MI 49516-6287
www.bakerbooks.com

Printed in the United States of America

Library of Congress Cataloging-in-Publication Data
Names: Powell, Kara Eckmann, 1970– author. | Griffin, Brad M., 1976– author.
Title: 3 big questions that change every teenager : making the most of your
    conversations and connections / Kara E. Powell and Brad M. Griffin.
Other titles: Three big questions that change every teenager
Description: Grand Rapids, Michigan : Baker Books, a division of Baker Publishing
    Group, [2021] | Includes bibliographical references.
Identifiers: LCCN 2020050073 (print) | LCCN 2020050074 (ebook) | ISBN
    9780801093388 (cloth) | ISBN 9781540901804 (paperback) | ISBN 9781493430314
    (ebook)
Subjects: LCSH: Church work with teenagers. | Christian teenagers—Religious life. |
    Identity (Psychology)—Religious aspects—Christianity.
Classification: LCC BV4447 .P6525 2021 (print) | LCC BV4447 (ebook) | DDC
    248.8/3—dc23
LC record available at https://lccn.loc.gov/2020050073
LC ebook record available at https://lccn.loc.gov/2020050074

To protect the privacy of those who have shared their stories with the authors, details and names have been changed.

The authors are represented by WordServe Literary Group.

21 22 23 24 25 26 27   7 6 5 4 3 2 1

To teenagers everywhere
who long for better answers

Contents

Part IV: What Difference Can I Make?

Part V: Questions Disrupted

Acknowledgments

We're always humbled when we get to the end of a writing project and list the voices and hands that contributed to making it a reality. While we cannot possibly thank everyone whose life touched this book, we're sure going to try to name many of them.

We absolutely couldn't have written this book without the twenty-seven teenagers who generously shared their stories of identity, belonging, and purpose. In order to protect their confidentiality, we will not name them (or the leaders who nominated them, to whom we're also grateful), but you will meet them by their aliases throughout the chapters that follow. We were just as dependent on the other members of the Fuller Youth Institute (FYI) interview team, who spent well over one hundred hours listening to young people tell their stories: Kat Armas, Macy Davis, Tyler Greenway, Jennifer Guerra Aldana, Garrison Hayes, Jane Hong-Guzmán de León, Helen Jun, and Andy Jung. Jane also managed the herculean process of identifying, tracking, matching, and scheduling interviewees across the project.

The transcription that made our interview analyses possible was capably handled by Stephen Bay, Rosa Cándida Ramírez, César Guzmán de León, Own Her, Helen Jun, Liz Jenkins, Sophia Kang, Adam Miller, Lauren Mulder, Lisa Nopachai, Joyce Oh, and Ahren Samuel.

Aaron Yenney led the literature review with persistence and endless curiosity, tracking down relevant sources along with interviewers Kat Armas and Helen Jun, plus Roslyn Hernández, Quanesha Moore, Gabriella (Gabi) Silva, and Sam Zheng Ning. Special thanks to Gabi for performing data analyses from interview transcripts. We're grateful to Tim Galleher and Giovanny Panginda for leading some of the focus groups with teenagers who helped shape our language.

We are indebted to the expert wisdom, keen insights, and course corrections provided by our project advisors, including Steve Argue, Scott Cormode, Joi Freeman, Jenny Pak, Montague Williams, and Almeda Wright. Jake Mulder helped shape this content as part of his overall leadership of the larger Living a Better Story project at FYI.

The original manuscript was dramatically improved by insights from many of the team members and advisors listed above along with thoughtful early feedback from Jen Bradbury, Rachel Dodd, Zach Ellis, Lisa Evans Hanle, Amy Fenton Lee, Lisette Fraser, Nica Halula, Jennifer Hananouchi, Chuck Hunt, Hannah Lee, Yulee Lee, Jeremy Morelock, Giovanny Panginda, Caleb Roose, Aaron Rosales, Daisy Rosales, Ahren Samuel, Ruby Varghese, and Kim Zovak. Thanks to Kristin Brussee for finessing our endnotes.

Along the way, we tried out ideas and explored concepts with conversation partners who pressed us to make this work stronger, from the earliest moments of the project to the final days before the manuscript was submitted. Whether over coffee, lunch, or Zoom, we were inspired by Manny Arteaga, Trey Clark, Joyce del Rosario, Matthew Deprez, Amanda Drury, Erin Dufault-Hunter, Benjamin Espinoza, Lauralee Farrer, Tommy Givens, Teesha Hadra, Kristen Ivy, Reggie Joiner, Chris Lopez, Megan Lundgren, Juan Martinez, Chris Neal, Tom Peitzman, Andy Root, Abigail Rusert, Matthew Russell, Josh Smith, Tamisha Tyler, Virginia Ward, and Amos Yong.

Special thanks to over fifty churches that participated in our Sticky Faith Innovation cohort and created new conversations and connections through a three-step process of compassion, creativity, and courage. Thanks also to Mountainside Communion for being a testing ground for so many ideas and practices, especially the youth ministry and pastoral teams.

We are grateful for the generous support of Lilly Endowment Inc., Tyndale House Foundation, and Sacred Harvest Foundation, and for their confidence that our work needed to be done for the sake of young people.

Our publishing team at Baker Books has provided the best partnership we could imagine. Profound appreciation goes to Brian Thomasson, Gisèle Mix, Mark Rice, Eileen Hanson, and the rest of the team, along with the support and representation of Greg Johnson and WordServe Literary.

The Fuller Youth Institute team is second to none. Their names appear across the lists above, and every one of them has strengthened what you will read in the pages that follow.

Finally, our families have inspired and challenged us and offered countless insights to this work. It's daunting to write a book about teenagers while raising three each with our respective spouses. Our kids have put up with not only our writing schedules but also dozens of "Hey, can I try an idea out with you?" and dinner-table conversations about research. They do an incredible job of keeping us real. And humble. Our spouses, Dave and Missy, deserve a special reward in heaven for making it possible for us to finish this book during months of unexpected (and seemingly unending) quarantine life. We are forever grateful.

PART I

QUESTIONS
BEGGING
FOR BETTER
ANSWERS

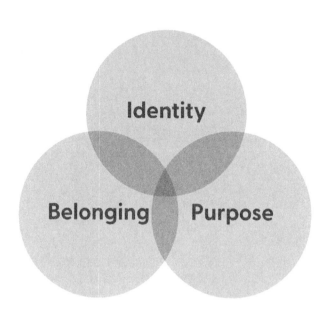

The Big Questions Every Teenager Is Asking

I've been slowly reflecting more on what it means to be a Christian, and I feel like I still don't know where exactly I fit into everything.

In middle school, I used to see everything as right and wrong because I was just learning the foundations. But as I eventually moved to high school and started learning critical thinking and that kind of thing, I've been slowly exploring the in-between areas. So I feel like I'm still trying to figure out my faith.

Lilly

As a twelfth grader, one student took a big risk and faced some big questions.

In ninth grade, she had been driven by one singular question: How can I successfully navigate my new twenty-five-hundred-student high school? Other than a few junior varsity swim meets when her fairly desperate coach dubbed her temporary (and last-minute) cocaptain, leadership wasn't in the picture. Surviving her growing homework load and shifting friendships were accomplishments enough.

As a tenth grader, with a year of classes and friendship under her belt, she started wondering, *How can I be a leader on campus without risking an election loss?* She found failure (public or not) unnerving. Gratefully, that question was answered when she applied for and was selected by teachers to serve as class secretary.

The next year she interviewed and was chosen by the student senate to be secretary of the school's student body. Then her English teacher asked her to be coeditor of the school paper. Between the newspaper and student government, she viewed herself—and was known to others—as a visible and active leader on campus.

Few eleventh graders had climbed so high up the school's student leadership ladder without winning a single election.

That streak ended senior year when she decided to run—in an *election*—for student body president. She and her campaign team gave away handfuls of candy, all plastered with creative slogans. While she still feared the humiliation of an election loss, underclassmen's widespread promises to vote for her made her optimistic she would triumph.

That hope disintegrated as soon as results were posted. Not only did she not win—she came in third. Out of three candidates.

This was no flubbed interview behind closed doors. This felt like public shaming. As adrenaline rushed through her body and she felt her face growing warm, one question flooded her mind: *Where can I hide?*

She drove home, ran upstairs to her bedroom, slammed the door, and curled under the covers. She had never tried this hard and failed this big. Half a dozen friends reached out to console her, but she was too embarrassed to talk.

Her bedspread was no shield against the core questions about herself, her relationships, and her future racing through her mind.

Who was she if she wasn't a student leader?

How could she face her friends, let alone the entire school?

And after this disgrace, could she ever lead anything again?

Every Teenager Is a Walking Bundle of Questions

Every teenager is a walking bundle of questions. For this student huddled in her bed, the questions were largely about leadership and risk. For students you know, the questions in their driver's seat may be about friends, race, money, grades, abuse, justice, sports, future, family, social media, or mental health.

Sometimes kids' questions leak out and are muttered aloud. More commonly, they remain bottled inside a teenager's curious mind and conflicted soul. Either way, we'll never activate this generation if we don't understand their most pressing questions.

You're likely reading this book because you want to understand teenagers and have better connections and conversations with them. You are a mentor, teacher, youth worker, small group leader, parent, stepparent, grandparent, pastor, church member, neighbor, aunt, or boss who wants to help address the questions of young people in general—and likely a few young people specifically.

At the Fuller Youth Institute, we love listening to teenagers' tough questions, as well as the (equally tough) questions *about* teenagers asked by churches, ministries, and families. Over the last couple of years, we've conducted surveys and focus groups with over twenty-two hundred teenagers, as well as in-depth multi-session interviews with twenty-seven youth group high school students nationwide (whom we will describe further in chapter 2). Among the questions tumbling through any teenager's mind at any time, the following questions often float to the top.

How Do I Manage Anxiety and Stress Better?

The two of us rarely go a day without a leader or parent asking us about young people's stress, anxiety, and depression.

That prevalence makes sense given that anxiety is the most common psychological disorder in the US, affecting nearly one-third of adolescents and adults in their lifetime.[1] So if you are a leader of twenty students, somewhere in the neighborhood of seven of them may suffer from a diagnosable anxiety disorder.

We'll further explore the causes, symptoms, and your best response to anxiety in chapters 4 and 5.

During the COVID-19 pandemic, mental health challenges skyrocketed in the US. According to the Centers for Disease Control and Prevention, anxiety tripled (from 8.1 percent to 25.5 percent) and depression almost quadrupled (from 6.5 percent to 24.3 percent). Approximately half of young adults ages eighteen to twenty-four during the pandemic were wrestling with anxiety or depression.[2]

Suicide is currently the second leading cause of death for US young people ages ten to twenty-four. What's more, approximately two out of every three young people who have suicidal thoughts never get help.[3]

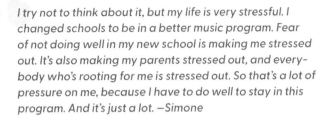

I try not to think about it, but my life is very stressful. I changed schools to be in a better music program. Fear of not doing well in my new school is making me stressed out. It's also making my parents stressed out, and everybody who's rooting for me is stressed out. So that's a lot of pressure on me, because I have to do well to stay in this program. And it's just a lot. —Simone

A few of the twenty-seven students we interviewed had contemplated or even taken specific steps toward killing themselves. One eleventh grader who's active in his church remembered feeling emotionally swallowed up by academic and social pressures: "On school days, I couldn't even make it until 10 or 11 a.m. My anxiety was crazy. It got to the point that I wanted to kill myself. I called a suicide hotline and was put in a hospital with security guards around my bed to make sure I wasn't going to harm myself. That was my lowest point."

Poignantly, the help he received during that hospitalization helped him peer behind the curtain of his emotions and discover what he ultimately longed for: "I finally realized in that hospital bed that I really didn't want to hurt myself. I just needed someone to be there for me."

Technology? We Don't Have Many Questions. We Kinda Get It.

If you're like us, whenever you have tech problems, you hand your device to the young person nearest you (resisting the impulse to throw it out the window instead). Today's teenagers have mastered—and are now pioneering—new paths forward in technology.

According to the latest research, nearly all (95 percent) of US teens have access to a smartphone, and about half say they are "almost constantly" on the internet.[4]

Almost three-fourths report often or sometimes checking for messages or notifications as soon as they wake up, and approximately four out of ten feel anxious when they do not have their cell phone with them.[5]

Roughly half of thirteen- to seventeen-year-olds are worried they spend too much time on their smartphones.[6]

Sixty-eight percent of young people who are active on social media have received support in tough times through those channels.[7]

With ubiquitous technology comes new temptations and conflict. In one survey of teenagers, 32 percent admitted to intentionally accessing online pornography; of these, 43 percent did so on a weekly basis.[8] During the course of our interviews, an upperclassman revealed his struggle with online pornography from sixth to ninth grade: "I was inundated with social media and introduced to all sorts of heinous stuff, you know, like porn. There was a whole bunch of mess that I got sucked into. No one knew what I was doing. I just deleted my online history. I was watching things I shouldn't have been watching. It was horrible for me."

> In chapters 4 and 6, we'll further explore the opportunities and challenges that technology introduces into young people's conversations and connections with you and our world.

Turning to another downside of technology, a junior we interviewed was one of the 15 percent of US high school students victimized by electronic bullying.[9] She was an African American minority at her school, and other students used her race as a weapon against her. No fists were thrown, but because she was different, insults were tossed her way both at school and in the digital world.

While this eleventh grader shared in specific detail about other aspects of her life, she didn't seem to want to give many details about this painful part of her history. I (Kara) asked her to tell me more about the bullying she had experienced. She paused and then gave a vague answer, "You know, name-calling. And people not wanting to be with me." She lowered her gaze, stared at the coffeehouse table in between us, sighed, and added one final, softly spoken, "Yeah . . ."

Our Generation Is Diverse, but How Do We Navigate All the Racial Pain in Our Country?

US Census statistics help us understand why this generation is so aware of ethnic and cultural diversity and why many are actively seeking racial justice and reconciliation. Today in the US, approximately half of those under eighteen are White and half are people of color;[10] one-fourth of that same age group are first- or second-generation immigrants.[11]

We might conclude from this data that if you're a leader, teacher, or mentor, about 50 percent of the children and teenagers you love and serve are likely to be White and 50 percent are likely to be from another ethnicity or two (or sometimes three or more). And if you're a parent, about half of your teenager's friends are White and half are likely young people of color.

However, America's racial reality is that our neighborhoods, schools, and churches remain relatively segregated. In some cases, students experience diverse classmates but go home to monocultural neighborhoods. For other teenagers, church is the most segregated environment of their

Social Location Matters

No matter our cultural background, we're all impacted by our social location.

By "social location," we mean the way we are shaped by our gender, race, ethnicity, social class, age, ability, religion, sexual orientation, and geography. While Brad is male and Kara is female, and we grew up in different parts of the country (Kara in suburban Southern California and Brad in rural Kentucky), our social locations today are fairly similar: we are both White, highly educated, middle to upper-middle class, straight, Protestant Christians who live in Los Angeles.

The way we lead our team, conduct research, and write this book are all influenced by social location. We can become more aware of those influences and at times compensate for them, but we can never fully distance ourselves from how our particular locations skew our perception. As practical theologians Juan Martinez and Mark Lau Branson warn, "Without self-awareness we are more prone to misunderstanding others and to underestimating the impact that our own heritage has on how we perceive and think and act."[a]

As we attempted to name how students' cultural experiences shape their quest for answers to their biggest questions, we didn't do this work alone. Our diverse and thoughtful team of researchers (whom you'll hear from throughout this book) helped us be more attentive to intersections of culture, race, gender, and other realities of social location.

Talking about race and culture is never simple. We often include the racial/ethnic background of interview participants when we attempt to capture their unique vantage points, but not every mention of a student will include this descriptor in order to avoid labeling. This may inevitably lead to assumptions and stereotypes both when we mention race and when we don't. If it's helpful to look up a particular young person's demographic background, please refer to the complete chart in appendix A.

a. Juan Martinez and Mark Lau Branson. *Churches, Cultures, and Leadership* (Downers Grove, IL: InterVarsity, 2011), 19.

week. And for still others, most every context in their lives is populated with people who look like them and share similar backgrounds. Often with fresh eyes, teenagers see the racial segregation and injustice surrounding them and are eager to work toward unity and healing.

In the midst of young people's varied ethnic and racial experiences, many have the opportunities to cross boundaries and build cultural bridges. Claudia is a seventeen-year-old Latina who loves traditional Mexican dishes but also enjoys Korean drinks and treats. She intentionally introduces her Latino friends to Korean cuisine and invites her Korean friends to enjoy Mexican food in her home and neighborhood. While this cultural exchange can at times create tension for Claudia and many students we interviewed, Claudia also enjoys watching both sets of friends try new foods. Claudia summarized: "Although I got some of their culture, I also got to share some of mine, and they actually love it. It's so fun."

How Do I Best Handle Gender Identity and Sexual Orientation?

In 2016, about ten million people, or 4.1 percent of the US adult population, identified as LGBTQ, which is a modest,

Half of Teenagers Struggle with Poverty

One in two US teenagers today are living in poverty or low-income households.[a] This income inequality creates a disparity that colors their search for answers to their pressing questions and hinders access to resources they need to navigate today's world.

a. Fifty-two percent of young people ages ten to nineteen: 16 percent below the poverty level and 36 percent in low-income households. United States Census Bureau, "Current Population Survey, Annual Social and Economic Supplement," 2018, http://www.census.gov/cps/data/cpstablecreator.html.

but noteworthy, increase from the 8.3 million (or 3.5 percent of adults) who said they were LGBTQ in 2012.[12] In one national study across generations, the youngest cohort surveyed (young adults ages eighteen to thirty-six) was by far the most likely to identify as LGBTQ (7.3 percent).[13] In addition, it's estimated that somewhere between 0.7 percent and 1.8 percent of US high school students identify as transgender.[14]

Gabriel is a recent graduate who describes himself as pansexual because "I will date someone for who they are." Taylor is a high school junior who prefers the pronoun *they*. Taylor describes themselves as "nonbinary, Christian, vegan, loving and empathetic, really gay, and quiet." When Taylor came out in middle school, many of Taylor's friends and family grew distant and seemed afraid of them. "My brother and I did not talk for like six months because he did not accept me. And that was really hard. But now he accepts me and stuff like that. I hear from other friends that he corrects people when they call me his sister because he knows how I feel about gender identity."

Today's young people who identify as straight and non-transgender are also navigating new questions with their gay, transgender, and nonbinary peers—including which terms to use and what they mean. As Steve, a high school senior from North Carolina, noted about one of his closer friends, "His girlfriend identifies as male, so he is pansexual. I respect what they both believe so I use the pronouns they want me to. I am not going to judge him, I'm not going to put him down. I am going to realize that his situation is different and respect that."

We'll further explore LGBTQ young people's identity journey in chapter 4 and their search for belonging in chapter 6.

When It Comes to Sex, How Do I Figure Out What's Best for Me?

The percentage of teenagers who report "ever having sex" has steadily dropped over the last decade—from 48 to 40—as has the percentage of those who are currently sexually active (from 35 to 29 percent).[15]

While these trends are promising, sexual temptations, hazards, and missteps remain part of young people's journeys. For today's tech-savvy students, sharing nude digital photos and videos is often an expected part of high school relationships.

During our interviews, one of our team members asked a sixteen-year-old who had dated one serious boyfriend in high school, "What is something you have learned about yourself because of that dating relationship?"

She responded, "I learned I have to be more self-confident."

The interviewer followed up, "How did that come up in your dating relationship?"

"Well, a lot of times, if you say no to something, the person you're dating kind of makes you feel bad about it. So you do it anyway. I wish I had been more confident so I could have stuck with my no instead of giving in."

How Can I Stay Safe at School? And Why Isn't More Being Done by Adults to Change Things?

Remember crouching under your school desk in elementary or high school during your annual earthquake or tornado drill (depending on which part of the country you grew up in)? Today's teenagers still do this drill, but campuses nationwide have added a second drill to their safety protocol.

Active-shooter drills.

The Sandy Hook Elementary school shooting was in 2012. The Parkland, Florida, shooting was in 2018. No wonder only 59 percent of fifth through twelfth graders report feeling safe at school.[16] A similar proportion (57 percent) of teenagers are worried about the possibility of a shooting happening at their school, with one out of four saying they are "very worried." This fear is higher among students of color.[17]

In chapter 10, we offer a conversation guide for processing local violence with teenagers.

Teenagers' underlying concern isn't just about school being dangerous but also that adults can't—or won't—protect them from violence. No longer waiting for adults, young people have been on the forefront of recent movements for legislative change addressing gun regulation across the country.

When It Comes to Drugs, Alcohol, and Vaping, What's Okay for Me to Try?

Experimentation is a hallmark of adolescence, and it's no surprise that drugs and alcohol are often in the mix among high schoolers. But the trends in this area are shifting. Overall, substance abuse is (wonderfully) declining among teenagers. The percentage of young people who report using illegal drugs has fallen (from 23 percent in 2007 to 14 percent in 2017), as has the percentage of those who have injected illegal drugs (from 2 to 1.5 percent over that same decade).

The percentage of tenth and twelfth graders who have consumed alcohol in the past year has seen a significant five-year drop—down to 38 percent and 52 percent, respectively.[18]

The glaring and alarming exception to these encouraging downturns is vaping, or the use of electronic cigarettes. Over one-third (35 percent) of twelfth graders have vaped nicotine in the last year, along with a distressing 17 percent of eighth graders.[19] Around 20 percent of tenth and twelfth graders have vaped marijuana in the past twelve months, which is more than double two years ago.[20]

In our interviews, we didn't ask directly about drugs, alcohol, or vaping, and few students voluntarily disclosed their own encounters. We were buoyed up when one senior who leads his school's Christian club noted that "a lot of students openly mock me for my faith in classes or refer to me as 'a dumb priest with his dumb Jesus.' I know these students are actively cutting and depressed. They are addicted to vaping. When they are in their most broken-down moments, at least three of them have come to me and asked, 'What makes you so happy?' That alone is like, wow."

How Is God Relevant to Me?

While the senior who leads his school's Christian club is known for his faith on campus, many churched young people, when asked how God is relevant to them, answer "not much at all."

For over fifteen years, we have been trying to answer questions about young people's faith through our research at the Fuller Youth Institute. Many of those questions come from leaders, parents, and mentors—people like you—who worry about the young people around them. Multiple studies indicate that 40 to 50 percent of young people—including those you know—who have been involved in a church or youth ministry will drift from God and the church after they graduate from high school.[21] So visualize the children and teenagers you care about most, and then imagine half of them leaving their faith behind in adulthood.

It's not just teenagers and young adults who are experiencing a spiritual decline. The proportion of US adults who describe themselves as Christians has dropped 12 percent in the past decade—down to 65 percent.

While that's disheartening, the data about young people is even more revealing. In those same surveys, only 49 percent of millennials, the youngest age group polled, described themselves as Christians, making them the least likely generation to do so.[22]

In a similar vein, the religious "Nones," or those who describe themselves as atheist, agnostic, or nothing in particular, now stand at 26 percent, up from 17 percent in 2009.

These statistics are daunting, but we wanted to hear more from young people themselves. Though the twenty-seven high school students we interviewed for this study were all involved in church youth groups, the centrality of their faith was certainly up for question. Some were exploring faith in creative and thoughtful ways, while others seemed to keep God compartmentalized.

In one of these interviews, our team member Tyler Greenway asked a midwestern high schooler, "How would you say your faith has shaped your sense of identity?"

We are privileged to lead the Fuller Youth Institute (FYI) alongside Jake Mulder, Yulee Lee, and one of the finest teams in the country. Every day our dedicated staff brings research to life as we work together to fulfill our mission to equip diverse leaders and parents so faithful young people can change our world.

To find out more about our work, resources, and training opportunities, please visit fulleryouthinstitute.org and subscribe to our email list today. There you'll also discover a host of resources accompanying this book.

There was a long pause before the student answered, "Not like a huge amount, but my faith like shapes part of who I am, I guess."

Tyler nudged him to offer specifics. "In what ways do you think it has shaped you?"

"Maybe it has made me more respectful."

Pressing in further, Tyler asked, "So how important would you say your faith is to you?"

"I would say it's pretty important."

Finally, Tyler offered, "So on a scale of 1 to 5, with 1 being not at all important and 5 being extremely important, how would you describe your faith?"

"Maybe like a 3. It's a big part of my life, but it's not my whole life, I guess."

Will Adults Please Stop Giving Me Answers to Questions I'm Not Asking?

Today's teenagers can access almost any information. They can instantaneously receive scores of possible answers to just about any question—plus a list of new ones. But they're also growing up in families and churches that shy away from some of their deepest questions about faith and meaning.

One of the reasons young people are drifting from faith is that churches aren't focused on the questions they care about most. Instead, we're pitching answers to questions that aren't anywhere near their strike zone.

We're too often stuck in questions that reflect what happened in the past.

Or we are missing what's unfolding in the present.

And we are afraid of what's to come in the future.

During a recent Fuller Youth Institute summit, the executive director from a national training organization shared about one high school student who yearned, "I wish the church would stop giving me answers to questions I'm not asking."

The specific questions that he and other teenagers most value might be unique to our time, but questions aren't new to God. By one count of the four Gospels, Jesus was asked 183 questions.[23]

That's remarkable, but what's even more remarkable is that Jesus himself asked 307 questions.

The question isn't whether faith is big enough to hold young people's questions. We know it is. The question is whether we will take the time to hear and honor them.

What's More Toxic Than Tough Questions?

One of our most counterintuitive findings over the years has been the role of doubt in teenagers' spiritual formation. In our research for *Sticky Faith*, 70 percent of former youth group students admitted to having significant questions about faith in high school.

Any temptation to panic can be calmed by this interesting research twist: those teenagers with doubts who felt the freedom and had the opportunity to express their questions actually showed *greater faith maturity*.[24]

Put more simply, it's not doubt that is toxic to faith—it's silence. Tough questions are most likely to sabotage faith when adults stifle them.

The 3 Big Questions Driving the Rest

While many questions are on the minds of today's teenagers, we've unearthed the three primary questions we believe undergird all the rest. These queries may not live right on the

As young people grapple with these deep internal questions, we see symptoms in their external attitudes and actions. No young person, let alone an entire generation, can be summarized with a few adjectives. Yet we've found these three descriptors helpful in understanding the teenagers around us. Maybe you'll likewise see that the teenagers in your life can often be

- *anxious* because of external stressors, which easily become internal pressure,
- *adaptive* as they adjust with creativity and agility to the new needs and opportunities they face, and
- *diverse* in their ethnicity, culture, socioeconomic status, gender identity, values, and worldview.

surface, but when we dig deep enough, we can trace their longings at the roots.

Almost every question young people are asking ultimately finds its genesis in these 3 big questions:

Who am I?

Where do I fit?

What difference can I make?

We've created shorthand phrasing to think about and explore these questions:

First, *identity*, which means *our view of ourselves.*

Then *belonging*, defined as *our connection with others.*

Finally, *purpose*, or *our contribution to the world.*

If it helps to see these organized in a table, the example below offers a start. We will continue to build on this table throughout the book.

Big Question	Focus	Description
Who am I?	Identity	Our view of ourselves
Where do I fit?	Belonging	Our connection with others
What difference can I make?	Purpose	Our contribution to the world

Throughout this book, you'll find images of three interlocking circles representing identity, belonging, and purpose. When we're focused on one of the three, that circle will be darker in the illustration. This is not only to orient you to where you are in the book but also to indicate that at any given time, one or another of the 3 big questions may take the lead in a young person's quest for answers. We've made the three circles overlapping because research with young people (others and our own) highlights that the three are interrelated and are best understood together.

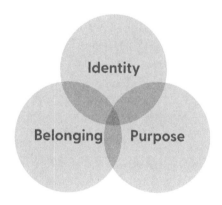

Our Fuller Youth Institute team talks about "identity, belonging, and purpose" so much that we refer to them as "IBP." If that shorthand helps you remember these three terms and talk about them with others, we encourage you to likewise adopt it. If you do, you'll fit right in with our team!

For much of the rest of this book, we'll be wrestling with these big questions, pinning down teenagers' current answers as well as better Christ-centered responses. For now, we want to warn you that while our research focused on young people, these questions cut across all generations.

They aren't just *young people* questions; they are *people* questions. They aren't relevant only to adolescents; they are relevant to the two of us. They are to you too. But for young people, the 3 big questions of identity, belonging, and purpose are at a constant, rolling boil.

Young People Need Adults Like You to Journey with Them in Their Big Questions

That high school senior huddled under her covers whose story started this chapter was certainly wrestling with these three questions.

Who am I if I'm not in student government? That's a
question of identity.

How can I face my friends when I'm so humiliated?
Sounds a lot like belonging.

What can I do to still have a meaningful senior year?
You guessed it—purpose.

Eventually, she left the safety of her bed and went downstairs to hugs from her mom, stepdad, and younger brother.

That helped. But she still felt discontented and disoriented.

Until Mike and Kristi, her youth pastor and small group leader, came by to talk.

They listened to her identity, belonging, and purpose questions and suggested answers bigger than anything she could see. She was especially surprised when Mike predicted, "Someday you're going to catch a vision for youth ministry. And then watch out."

As he had anticipated, she started hanging around the church more, and even joined the student leadership team. (To her relief, no election was required.)

By the end of her senior year, she was running that team.

During her college summers, she served in the youth ministry as a volunteer and then as a paid intern.

Her youth pastor was right. God gave her a vision for young people. And thirty years later, she's still in youth ministry.

You've perhaps figured out that I (Kara) was that defeated and disgraced high school senior. Mike was my youth pastor, and Kristi was my small group leader. They walked beside me in high school and beyond as I stumbled and crawled toward God's better answers for my identity, belonging, and purpose. (And yes, I'm tearing up as I type this.)

I wouldn't be doing what I do, or writing this book, if they hadn't patiently and prayerfully journeyed beside me. (Now the tears are streaming down my cheeks. Good thing I'm writing at home and my teenagers are out.)

You can be a Mike or a Kristi.

You can be that adult who sees God's potential for a young person's identity, belonging, and purpose when all they see is defeat and dead ends.

We wrote this book for any adult who cares about teenagers (meaning thirteen- to eighteen-year-olds; roughly middle school and high school), or a particular teenager. We had such a wide pool of fellow learners in mind that no matter your life stage or role, you are almost certainly one of us! Throughout these pages, we will highlight those insights and ideas that are even more relevant for families or for ministry leaders.

Whether you're married or single, paid or volunteer, church or parachurch, a parent, stepparent, foster parent, or grandparent, an empty nester or nonparent, you can have better connections and conversations with teenagers as they trailblaze toward God's best answers.

We know you can do it.

We're cheering for you.

And for young people.

REFLECT and APPLY

1. What questions were most pressing for you when you were a teenager?

2. How were those questions perhaps linked with your deeper quest for identity, belonging, and purpose?

3. How, if at all, did an adult(s) journey with you and point you to Jesus' better answers to those 3 big questions? What did that adult do well? What do you wish they had done differently?

4. What pressing questions (from this chapter or elsewhere) are being asked by the young people you're closest to? Which do you feel inadequate to answer right now?

5. How do you imagine those questions might be connected to the 3 big questions of identity, belonging, and purpose?

6. What excites you about the prospect of better connections and conversations with young people as they pursue identity, belonging, and purpose? What intimidates you or makes you a bit nervous?

Learning to Listen for Answers

BRAD: Is there anything else before I stop recording, about anything that we've talked about or something that has come to mind, that you didn't get a chance to say?

DANIEL: Not really. Just that I am going to miss these talks. I really like doing this one-on-one thing. It's really cool.

Janelle is a junior in high school. She's friendly, easy to talk with, and thoughtful. Her brother is one of her closest friends; he makes her feel good about herself. She often hangs out with his friends because they cause "less drama" than the girls she knows at school.

For a period of time when Janelle was younger, her family experienced homelessness, moving from shelter to shelter. After her mom married her stepdad, their housing stabilized. She has lived in the same apartment for a few years now and likes her neighborhood. When asked to share a photo of something that reminds her of belonging, Janelle shared a picture from her phone of her front door—because home is where she feels safe. One of her dreams for the future is not to live in an apartment. Someday she'd like to live in a yellow house, with a yard where kids can play.

Like many teenagers in her generation, Janelle wrestles with anxiety. She remembers several intense experiences with mental health struggles in middle and early high school.

> I didn't know it was anxiety at the time. I was always sick, but I would pretend I was fine, like there was nothing wrong. My therapist now says it was a coping skill. I wouldn't let myself eat if I was anxious. I would tell my mom that I had already eaten so she wouldn't be worried. Or I would tell her that I had friends I would hang out with, because I didn't want her to be worried that I wasn't making friends. I would hide in the bathroom to cry several times a day, and sometimes have panic attacks.

Eventually, Janelle was diagnosed with an anxiety disorder, and she found the help she needed.

It's important to Janelle to talk with other people about mental health. Particularly as an African American, she thinks it's vital to share her story with other Black students to destigmatize getting help.[1]

Listening for the 3 Big Questions in Janelle's Story

Like all teenagers, Janelle is working out her identity, belonging, and purpose while navigating the daily ups and downs of adolescence. As we spent more time with her, we were able to understand Janelle's own unique journey in answering the 3 big questions.

Identity: Who Am I?

"Compassionate" is the way Janelle describes herself, in part because it's an important quality she looks for in a friend. She says her own tough experiences have given her more compassion for other people who are struggling.

Her parents see her as confident and smart. She's self-assured, but others' opinions also really matter. This year she started serving as a leader in her school's Black Student Union. But painfully, Janelle is also targeted with the racial stereotype of not being "Black enough" because she gets "really good grades." Grappling with this discrimination, Janelle asserts that other kids "shouldn't assume Black people are not smart."

At the same time, she feels continual pressure—internally and externally—to perform academically. "I feel like I have to do everything so perfect." Janelle constantly lives in the intersectionality of her identity markers: young, Black, female, smart, confident, anxious.[2]

Belonging: Where Do I Fit?

Janelle thinks that for most people her age, friends are their safe place. But for her, it's family and church. Her apartment's living room is where she overall feels safest, with church being a close second. She loves her church and feels a deep sense that she is part of the community. Janelle talked about one leader in particular who has really been there for her: "She's always checking in on me."

Janelle thinks about belonging "*all* the time. I think that's the big thing for me, but I think that's a big thing for a lot of people. You want to know if you really fit in there, if they really like you coming along or just invited you because they felt bad."

Purpose: What Difference Can I Make?

Janelle gains a sense of purpose from serving at church, especially in children's ministry. Working with kids at her church's summer camp raised her confidence last year. She shared, "I was asked to do so many things outside my comfort zone, but that was a time when I felt happy. I was doing things for God."

Thinking ahead to her future, Janelle offered, "I think I want to be a child development clinical psychologist. I want to work with kids." She went on to share, "I would like to impact people the way my psychologist and therapist impacted me. They made things a lot easier for me."

The Research behind the Stories

Janelle was part of the interview study we mentioned in chapter 1. Our research team wanted to uncover teenagers' current answers to their biggest questions. We used an approach called "narrative analysis" to explore the 3 big questions of identity, belonging, and purpose.[3]

Connecting the Dots among Identity, Belonging, and Purpose

You may see hints in Janelle's story of the interplay among identity, belonging, and purpose. We found quite a bit of overlap in students' responses to our questions—sometimes purpose sounded like identity, or identity like belonging. We often found that the pursuit of belonging leads the way among teenagers' 3 big questions.

Our research team sat down one-on-one with twenty-seven teenagers from a wide variety of backgrounds for three consecutive interviews. Each was nominated by a youth ministry leader as a young person who might be willing to talk about their life and experiences of faith, but some were more involved in church than others. We asked dozens of questions for up to two hours at a time. The ten interviewers roughly represented the cultural and geographic diversity of the sample.[4] (Use appendix A as a quick reference for each participant's name—we've changed them all—and demographics.) See the illustrations on pages 48–49 for a full picture of our interviewee demographics.[5]

In addition to the two of us, the interview team for this project included Kat Armas, Macy Davis, Tyler Greenway, Jennifer Guerra Aldana, Garrison Hayes, Jane Hong-Guzmán de León, Helen Jun, and Andy Jung.

Over one hundred hours of interviews were transcribed, and our team pored over the transcripts and reports from each interviewer. We met together periodically and in an all-day gathering to explore themes and share highlights.[6] We also reached out to more teenagers (beyond the interviewees) through twelve focus groups to field our ideas and learn from their helpful correctives.[7]

Alongside interviews, a literature review team explored themes of identity, belonging, purpose, faith formation, Generation Z, and narrative studies. Over one hundred cross-disciplinary academic and popular sources were consulted in this process.[8]

Finally, we compared what we heard in these in-depth interviews with data from 2,092 youth ministry student surveys from our related innovation project[9] that focused on identity, belonging, and purpose.

Race/ Ethnicity

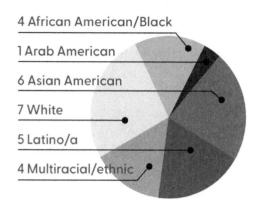

4 African American/Black

1 Arab American

6 Asian American

7 White

5 Latino/a

4 Multiracial/ethnic

Gender

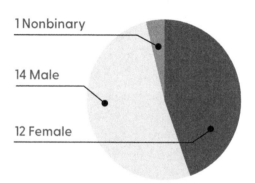

1 Nonbinary

14 Male

12 Female

Geography

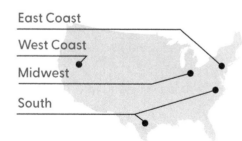

East Coast

West Coast

Midwest

South

Denomination

19 TEENAGERS FROM
11 different Protestant denominations

8 nondenominational churches

Socioeconomics

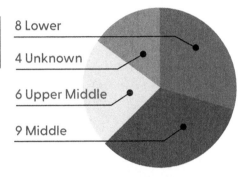

8 Lower

4 Unknown

6 Upper Middle

9 Middle

Community Type

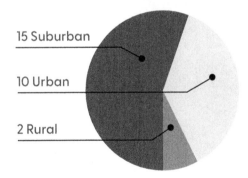

15 Suburban

10 Urban

2 Rural

Grade in School

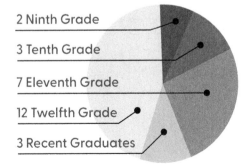

2 Ninth Grade

3 Tenth Grade

7 Eleventh Grade

12 Twelfth Grade

3 Recent Graduates

We did all this listening so you could hear young people in their own words—and hear them better.[10]

Why Listening to Real Young People Matters

> The beginning of love for others is learning to listen to them. God's love for us is shown by the fact that God not only gives God's Word, but also lends us God's ear. . . .
>
> Christians who can no longer listen to one another will soon no longer be listening to God either.
>
> Dietrich Bonhoeffer[11]

One of the reasons we conducted this research was to help adults like you—and ourselves—move beyond assumptions to truly connect with teenagers.

Assumptions keep us at a distance.

Assumptions lead to judgment. We judge across generations all the time, and this judgment allows us to comfortably dismiss what we experience as *different* by declaring it *wrong*.

Young people feel this judgment. Karie, a freshman, can tell when adults are guided by assumptions. She shared the following with Jane Hong-Guzmán de León, her interviewer:

KARIE: So, for example, an adult might say, "Oh yeah, it's just because you guys have your phones," and just stupid things like that.

JANE: What are some of the common misconceptions?

KARIE: That we are addicted to social media, or social media is so bad for us. There are certainly cons to it, but there are also pros, and I feel like they do not see that. It's not right to blame everything on how we use social media.

Research Snapshot

100+
Hours of interviews[1]

27
Teenagers interviewed

2,200
Teenagers represented through interviews, surveys, and focus groups

13
Distinct ethnic backgrounds[2]

1. See appendix B for the full list of over 170 questions we asked each young person!
2. African American, Caribbean, Chinese, Egyptian, Filipino, Japanese, Korean, Latino/a, White (European American), African American/Chinese, African American/Korean, African American/White, Latina/Korean.

Karie wasn't the only one to express this sentiment. Here are a couple of other thoughts from teenagers we asked about adults' misperceptions:

> Teenagers are underestimated a lot. People are uncomfortable talking about conflict or something controversial in front of teenagers, but we aren't surprised by it. It's weird when adults act like we're less, or like we don't know what we're talking about. Even small comments. We notice.

> Ask teenagers about something you wouldn't usually ask them, even questions that are uncomfortable. Teenagers have a lot more to offer. We have real opinions. We have beliefs and experiences and thoughts about things going on that adults might not be aware of. Things have changed since you were in high school.

Indeed, things have changed since we were in high school. Whether that was more than twenty-five years ago (like both of us; okay, for Kara, it's actually more than thirty) or even just a few years ago, things are different for today's students.

Truly listening to young people pushes us past our tendencies to assume and judge.

Listening brings us closer.

Listening helps us forge a new path across the generational impasse.

But we can't stop there. Listening opens us up to the next step. It makes *empathy* possible.

Empathy Changes Everything

In our previous research studying churches that are Growing Young (see fulleryouthinstitute.org/growingyoung for details and resources), we identified empathy as one of six core commitments found in churches that effectively engage young people. Among all the things churches were doing well—developing a culture of "keychain" (shared) leadership, taking Jesus' message seriously, nurturing warm community, prioritizing young people everywhere, and being the best local and global neighbors—intergenerational empathy played a unique and powerful role by weaving through the other commitments.

We defined *empathy* in *Growing Young* as "*feeling with* young people . . . sitting on the curb of a young person's life, celebrating their dreams and grieving over their despair."[12] Since that time, countless adults have asked us for more help with understanding empathy and putting it into practice. So we'll add to our original description this way: we practice empathy when we *notice* and *care*.

EMPATHY = NOTICE + CARE

Noticing is reading someone else's emotions. Caring is responding to those emotions with feelings of our own.[13]

Taking another's perspective increases our ability to understand them and helps us avoid judgment and stereotypes. It humanizes them as we see reality through their eyes—if only for the moment—rather than othering them and holding them at a distance. It steps into their shoes for a few paces on the road. Empathy increases our drive to help others rather than ignore their pain.

Empathy isn't just for tragedies and bad days. This is a common misconception, one we've perpetuated ourselves by the way we couch empathy as a response to pain. It *is* that, but it's also so much more. In all days and in the midst of all

Othering may be a new term for you. Whenever we speak to or about someone in a way that treats them as inherently different from ourselves, we are othering. This move marginalizes someone or entire people groups by contrasting them against our version of normal (which usually looks a lot like us). Think of it as anything that communicates, "I'm normal; you're not."[a]

emotions, empathy pushes past the superficial and creates a safe space for the real story to emerge.

Empathy can be hard because it forces us to break old habits. In our past efforts at FYI to help build empathy for teenagers' search for identity, belonging, and purpose,[14] we used to ask youth leaders to spend time in the spaces where young people gather, such as sporting events, skate parks, and coffee shops. We speculated that asking leaders to observe at a distance would be less intimidating for adults and less intrusive for young people.

We hoped leaders' observations would trigger empathy. But that's not what happened. While it was helpful to see young people beyond the church walls, most adults tended to reinforce stereotypes when they described what they learned:

"They're always on their phones."

"They are present but not really there."

"They spend too much money on silly things."

"They just seem lonely."

Hoping to move beyond these shallow assumptions, we next asked leaders to *talk* with young people instead. We

a. To explore the use of othering in American literature, see Toni Morrison, *The Origin of Others* (Cambridge, MA: Harvard University Press, 2017).

gave them question prompts to use (a lot like the conversations permeating chapters 5, 7, and 9). We reminded them to withhold judgment and ask for clarity, especially with cultural references or teenage slang. This approach produced remarkably different interpretations. Leaders were struck by how distant they had become from young people's real lives. Phrases beginning with "I didn't know . . . ," "I never realized . . . ," and "I now see . . ." signaled a shift toward empathy.

You're likely nodding along. Chances are good that you already know this intuitively. You're probably naturally empathetic toward teenagers—otherwise, you wouldn't have picked up this book. Here's your invitation to go deeper. Take another step closer. Intentionally practice *noticing* and *caring*.

NOTICE: Can You See Me? Can You Hear Me?

"Being heard is so close to being loved that for the average person, they are almost the same."[15] When our friend Mike Park, a church-planting pastor in New York City, shared this quote with a group of leaders at one of our innovation summits, the room fell quiet.

We try a lot of things in our churches to attract or engage young people. Sometimes these efforts are fruitful. But if we aren't creating environments and relationships in which young people can be heard and seen, we may be wasting our time. We're missing true conversation and connection.

Many of us can call to mind the people who extended us this gift while we were growing up. I (Brad) remember the two teachers who really saw me. Mrs. Patty Davis was the first grade teacher I needed—the perfect combination of authority and love. She sent me to the principal's office with a pink slip for talking too much. But she also tended to my social exclusion, my nervous tick, and the fact that I was lagging behind in reading. She knew I was growing up on a farm out in the country and noticed that I found it hard to fit in with town kids who swam at the same club and played in the same neighborhoods with other classmates.

I don't remember why I had trouble with reading, but I remember the paperback book about a boy and his duck that I wanted to read over and over during quiet time. And I still remember the smell of the old-school photocopy ink on my personal version of that book, which Mrs. Davis took time to create so I could read it at home.

I remember these things because Mrs. Davis saw me.

Listen for Answers—Listen for Stories

We've used the term *stories* a few times already in this chapter. Teenagers—and all of us—answer the 3 big questions with stories. In this book, we will talk a lot about stories or narratives as a way to make meaning.

The way teenagers tell a story likely tells you something about how they see themselves. Here's where each of us comes in. Psychologists tell us that engaged listening helps teenagers make sense of their stories.[a] As we listen empathetically and give feedback, we help young people become narrators of their identity, belonging, and purpose journeys.[b] We think you have what it takes to be this kind of adult in a young person's life.

---

a. This is because stories we tell about ourselves are products of both the speaker *and* the listener, a process known as "coconstruction." Engaged listening includes being attentive, supportive, and challenging, and offering interpretation. Laura Ferrer-Wreder and Jane Kroger, "Identity as Life Story: Narrative Understandings of Adolescent Identity Development," in *Identity in Adolescence: The Balance between Self and Other* (New York: Routledge, 2020), 112.

b. Monisha Pasupathi, "The Social Construction of the Personal Past and Its Implications for Adult Development," *Psychological Bulletin* 127, no. 5 (2001): 651–72.

Then in middle school, there was Mrs. Debbie Dwyer. Starting in sixth grade, she saw something in me that others didn't: the potential to take my over-the-top personality and extra-loud voice and channel both toward public speaking. At her invitation, I joined the speech and drama team and never looked back. (I'm guessing she heard me more than she anticipated!)

While God used that training to prepare me for the speaking, preaching, and teaching I do now, the real power of Mrs. Dwyer's influence reached far beyond a skill set. In a season when I was experiencing intense social rejection, she never once made me feel left out, weird, or alone.

She didn't just see something *in* me—she saw *me*. That gift profoundly shaped who I am today.

CARE: Putting Empathy into Action

"What am I good at?"

This text from fifteen-year-old Noah caught Damon off guard. Damon, a youth leader at Noah's church, could think of lots of answers. So he shot back a list: "You're good at relating with people, an influencer, an artist, a sharp student."

"I don't have any real talent, though," came the reply.

Damon responded with another list of accolades and encouragement. More self-rejection followed from Noah. The cycle continued.

One of Noah's last statements in the conversation was "I just want to know why I'm not enough right now." And then Noah stopped texting Damon.

Damon couldn't figure out what had gone wrong in this conversation. At every turn, he had sought to encourage

Noah. He tried reassurances. He tried replacing negative self-talk with truth. What happened?

Damon shared this story with a friend at a training I (Brad) was leading for a group of youth ministry leaders. In the session, we were talking about the power of empathy for young people. A friend at Damon's table read the text thread and shook his head. Then he said something that floored Damon.

"You never made him feel heard. You just tried to fix it. That's not what he needed."

Despite his best intentions to help Noah, Damon missed what Noah may have wanted most in that moment: someone to empathize with what he was *actually feeling*. Damon reflected, "I seemed more interested in fixing the problem than trying to wrestle with the questions with him. I began hammering away at his feelings, hoping to change his mind rather than hear his heart."

Maybe you've had a similar experience. You're trying to care, but it backfires. Here are a few tips for next time.

Tell Me More

I don't know about you, but I often find myself in conversations with young people that bump along awkwardly and end abruptly. As one of the ministry volunteers at my church recently shared, "I am apparently terrible at getting more than one-word answers in conversation with most of the guys." Can you relate?

Me in the past: "How was your baseball game this weekend?"

Teenager: "Good."

Me: "Cool."

That's usually how it ended.

Our team has also created a series of brief intergenerational conversation tool kits that address particular cultural realities, including African American, Asian American, and Latino/a young people. Explore the options (plus bilingual versions in Spanish, Korean, and Mandarin) at fulleryouthinstitute.org/multicultural.

Until I started using a key phrase FYI teammate Steve Argue has championed for years. In conversations and connections with young people, try using this simple three-word invitation: *Tell me more.*

Memorize those words right now.

In the baseball conversation above, a "tell me more about that" might still yield a short answer. But sometimes it opens enough of a crack for an adult to peer inside the elusive experience of the reserved teenager. And with older students who may be jaded by how little adults seem to want to know about them, "tell me more" can be a relational game changer.

There are all kinds of variations on this approach. We could ask for more specificity, like "What was good about the game?" or "What made it fun?"

Steve will often say, "The first question isn't as important as the second or third question." That's because the first question we ask comes from our agenda; what follows emerges from the unfolding conversation.

Match Your Words with Your Body Language

We say as much with our expressions, attention, and posture as we do with our words. But I (Brad) confess that I sometimes struggle with empathetic nonverbal communication. It's not unusual for Kara to say in a meeting, "I can't tell by your affect how you're feeling." When I am processing information and considering what to say, I can forget to tell my face to keep up. The problem is, other people need cues from our expressions. They need to know whether to keep talking or to shut up. They need to know whether they're being understood or misinterpreted. Our faces help fill in the blanks beyond what we are saying out loud.

The coronavirus pandemic of 2020—and the subsequent shift from in-person to virtual gatherings—gave many of

It's Personal

What does every kid need at least one adult in their life to know? Our good friends at Orange have been wrestling with this question as they help church leaders partner with the home to form the faith of children and teenagers. In their own work on identity, belonging, and purpose, Virginia Ward, Reggie Joiner, and Kristen Ivy identified the following five empathetic questions that every young person wonders about any adult who cares about them.[a]

- *Do you know my name?* This makes me feel noticed, memorable, and honored.
- *Do you know what matters to me?* This communicates my unique worth.
- *Do you know where I live?* This makes me feel understood and accepted.
- *Do you know what I've done?* This lets me know I'm loved despite my mistakes.
- *Do you know what I can do?* This reminds me I am significant and have potential.

In your next conversation with a young person, imagine these questions hiding behind the eyes looking back. The more you understand, the deeper your influence on the young person in front of you.

a. You can explore these questions further in Virginia Ward, Reggie Joiner, and Kristen Ivy, *It's Personal: Five Questions You Should Answer to Give Every Kid Hope* (Atlanta: Orange Books, 2019).

us new opportunities to see what we look like in meetings, ministry gatherings, and one-on-one conversations. While I prefer to hide my own self-view and focus on the other people onscreen, sometimes in these digital encounters I watch my face to see my reactions and learn how others might be experiencing them. Occasionally I even find myself practicing empathetic responses and trying to avoid expressions that could miscommunicate.

Perhaps you're using videoconferencing enough to try the same exercise for a week. Maybe you can practice empathetic expressions in the mirror every morning while you're getting ready. Or over the next month, choose one expression you want to offer a young person in your interactions and look for natural opportunities to do so.

Obstacles to Empathy: Two Pairs of Extremes

When it comes to relating to young people like Janelle, whom we met at the start of this chapter, we all fall into common traps that short-circuit our attempts at connection. These traps can be grouped in two sets of extremes.

"When I Was Your Age" versus "You're So Different from Me"

It can be easy to assume we have too much or too little in common across generations. Let's start with "When I was your age." This statement rarely precedes an empathetic response. Think about the tone in your voice when those words slide out: critical, judgmental, pejorative. We would do well to remove the phrase from our vocabulary altogether.

Why? Here's the truth. We may have been teenagers once, but we've never been "their age."

We can remember what it was like to be a teenager, but we've never been teenagers in *their* world.

On the flipside of "When I was your age" is another fallacy: "You're so different from me." We often assume that young people are so different—so *other*—from us that we couldn't possibly understand them.

One leader from Tennessee observed:

> Honestly, I think empathy may be our biggest challenge. It is super easy for me—a child of the '80s and '90s—to judge technology and social media and say they are the biggest hindrance to spiritual formation. But the reality is that I just want something to blame. It helps to have technology as a scapegoat. That's not just a speed bump to empathy; it's a roadblock!

Rather than simply critique kids' tech habits, we can empathize with a need we all share regardless of age: *relationships*. When you were in high school, you may have spent evenings at home in your bedroom on the family telephone—perhaps with a long curly cord plugged into a wall—talking to your best friend (with whom you had just spent all day at school). Your parents may have even decided to pay extra for call waiting so other calls could get through during your hours-long conversations. Or maybe you came of age in the brief-but-exciting pager phase, when cryptic messages came beeping through your hip-side device to make you feel important and needed. Perhaps you had an early Nokia or Razr cell phone—not yet "smart," but it definitely helped you stay connected with your friends.

You get the point.

You've been there. Relationships matter—to all of us, but especially to adolescents (which is why this book devotes an entire section to the big question of belonging). Tap into your own memories from the past to strengthen your empathy and build deeper connections with the young people in front of you today.

"What You Need to Do" versus "This Is Totally under Your Control"

In this second pair of extremes, we either rescue young people from their problems or abandon them to figure things out on their own.

We frequently feel like we have advice to give teenagers. That's normal. We have lived longer, experienced more, and gained wisdom from the road. But in the face of a dilemma, if we jump in too quickly with a "what you need to do" suggestion, we risk communicating that a teenager isn't capable of handling problems on their own. We rob them of the value of sorting things out, making decisions, and learning from failure.

The opposite response can also be crippling. "This is totally under your control" sounds empowering on the surface (and when a young person is ready for it, can actually be empowering). But putting the entire responsibility on a teenager to solve a problem can sound like the young person is to blame. If they had only tried harder or not made a mistake or avoided a situation, they would not have ended up here. And now they—on their own—have to dig their way out.

Continuing Our Own Search for Identity, Belonging, and Purpose

While "when I was your age" may not be very empathetic, it doesn't mean we should never revisit our experiences.

Getting close to teenagers can remind us of our own quest for identity, belonging, and purpose—maybe too much.

It turns out we adults need to do the work too.

Sometimes we struggle to really be there for teenagers because we have unresolved questions and toxic stories we're telling ourselves. When we try to connect with a teenager, we find ourselves wondering, *Will they like me? Will they listen to me? Will I really make a difference?*

Perhaps especially for those of us who are parents, our kids' journeys to discover identity, belonging, and purpose affect our own in surprising ways.

All three of my (Kara's) kids went to the same school from kindergarten through eighth grade. We had nine great years with more or less the same kids and families through elementary and middle school.

Which made the process of making new friends in ninth grade especially jarring—for me.

Our kids did just fine. I was the one riddled with anxiety and insecurity. Especially with Nathan, our oldest. When I picked him up those first few late August days at his new high school, I was eager to hear who he had lunch with, who he sat next to in class, and who he thought might become a real friend.

Truth be told, I was far *too* eager. And this is even more embarrassing, but I feel safe enough to admit it: I took comfort that Nathan seemed to be connecting with the "popular" kids.

Two weeks into ninth grade, Nathan and the rest of his class went away on a camping trip. When Nathan returned, he gave me a recap of what had happened. Apparently, both nights he hung out with the more popular kids. But when they started teasing and making fun of other kids, that bothered Nathan. He told me over dinner, "The most popular kids are kinda jerks. I think I'd rather hang out with the kids who are in the 'next tier.'"

I was proud of my boy for looking past popularity in choosing his buddies. But I wasn't proud of my own reaction. That night I confessed to my husband, Dave, "I'm glad Nathan's choosing character first. But I have to admit I wish he was still hanging out with the popular kids."

Why did I care more about Nathan hanging out with the popular kids than he did? Because as I journeyed alongside Nathan in his search for belonging, my own insecurities about friendship were heightened. Subconsciously, I hoped that if he received a stamp of approval from the right students, that would somehow reverberate three decades into my past and make my teenage self feel more welcomed and valued.

So many of us try to lead or love from a place of deficit. Doing our own work on identity, belonging, and purpose can open us up to empathize with young people on a whole new level.

How do the 3 big questions bubble to the surface for you these days?

What triggers your insecurity?

What does it look like for you to lean into God's truths about your identity, belonging, and purpose?

While we will invite you to look back at your own story throughout this book, it might be helpful to pause right now and name how you're answering the questions of identity, belonging, and purpose today. Good self-reflection can help till the soil of empathy for others. We've included some questions at the end of this chapter to get you started.

Where We're Going: Current Answers and Christ-Centered Answers

Janelle's faith grounds her through the ups and downs of her journey toward identity, belonging, and purpose. One of her go-to Scripture passages is Psalm 139:14. Reflecting on its significance, Janelle shared:

> That's my favorite one. It says I'm "fearfully and wonderfully made." It's really important to me. I think, especially when I was going through mental illness, I felt like, why would God make me like this? Or when we were in shelters, or like, all this stuff, why would God do this? But that verse helped me know that he makes things and he thinks they're good. I think it makes me look at the good and bad things that I see in myself, that they are all there for a reason.

Janelle has several adults in her life who have taken time to listen well and empathize with her quest to answer the 3 big questions in light of her faith. In chapter 3 we turn our attention to the ways she and other teenagers in our interviews talked about faith and how we might help them imagine new ways of answering the big questions.

Chapters 4, 6, and 8 will strengthen our "notice and care" muscles by digging deeply into what we learned in our research about current answers to identity, belonging, and purpose.

Chapters 5, 7, and 9 will explore more life-giving faith-filled answers. We'll offer all sorts of practical ideas to launch conversations and connections that can move the young people in your life toward Jesus' better answers.

REFLECT and APPLY

1. What are your go-to stereotypes and assumptions about teen-agers? (Be honest!)

2. What is something you've been surprised by when talking with a teenager that pushed against your assumptions?

3. List a handful of topics you would like to learn more about from a teenager in your life. Start each topic with, "Tell me more about ..."

4. Name one or two adults who truly saw and heard you when you were growing up. How did they *notice* and *care*? If you didn't have an adult like that in your life, reflect on how that impacted you during those years.

5. What triggers your insecurity about identity, belonging, and purpose these days? How might you do some work on the 3 big questions for yourself?

Jesus Offers
Better Answers

Usually when I describe God to my friends, I describe God as a best friend. Like someone who is always there for you. Sometimes I describe him as a father, but that is sometimes a sore topic. When you think of a father you think of your own, so it's not always the best example. So when I talk about God, I usually describe him as a friend. It's easier to understand, because almost everyone has at least one person they consider a friend.

Janelle

Samuel has been part of the same church his entire life, as has much of his extended Asian American family. "Church and family always went hand in hand for me," he said the first time he met with me (Brad) to share his story. He continued, "I always had people I knew. Church was never a place I didn't want to be."

Today he's a leader both in his youth group and in a Christian club at his public school. Now a senior, Samuel is looking at Christian colleges and working around twenty hours a week in fast food to save up for tuition. Friday night youth group is the highlight of Samuel's week. He loves connecting with other students and leaders, the small groups after the message, and closing worship when students can receive prayer. "We all know what each other's going through. And if you're involved, you're really involved, you're really part of the community."

Samuel talks about a turning point his sophomore year that made his faith real—when he decided to stop wearing so many "different hats" and chose to wear his "faith hat" consistently. He changed friend groups, distancing himself from damaging relationships. He spent weeks eating lunch alone in a classroom, using lunchtime to pray and sort things out. "It was a safe place for me. I was really broken, but it was really good because I used that brokenness to grow." Now he speaks of that time as "growing relationally with God. And just finding myself."

The more Samuel shared with me, the clearer it became that his faith is very real and integrated into most every area of his life. When he talks about the 3 big questions, his answers are grounded in Jesus and clearly shaped by his family and church.

How Does the Gospel Respond to the Big Questions Today's Teenagers Are Asking?

In chapter 1, we wrote that teenagers often wonder, *How is God relevant to me?* We heard from a student who reflected that faith was "a big part of my life, but it's not my whole life, I guess." In our experience, many young people are a lot more like that student than Samuel. Faith is in the picture, but it's not integrated. And all too often, it feels like a compartmentalized extra more than a life essential.

Empathizing with today's teenagers is the first step to helping them answer their big questions of identity, belonging, and purpose. The next step is to ask, If these are the biggest questions, what does the good news of Jesus Christ say in response?

Young people need new plotlines, new mantras to say to themselves over and over about who they are, where they fit, and what difference they can make. These new Christ-centered stories can replace teenagers' incomplete or toxic narratives, empowering them to live out more freeing answers to their most pressing questions.

We believe this is the heart of discipleship.[1]

We find it helpful to view the 3 big questions, current answers, and Christ-centered answers together in a table. We will continue to build on this table throughout the book as we explore identity, belonging, and purpose in the lives of today's teenagers.

Big Question	Focus	Description	Current Answers	Christ-Centered Answer
Who am I?	Identity	Our view of ourselves		
Where do I fit?	Belonging	Our connection with others		
What difference can I make?	Purpose	Our contribution to the world		

The Gospel Isn't Thin, but Sometimes Teenagers' Jesus-Answers Are

In our interviews with students like Samuel, we asked a lot of questions about faith and church. One of those questions was "What does it mean, to you, to be a Christian?"

We noticed three themes in students' answers: behavior, belief, and relationship. At first glance, these themes were unsurprising, but what did catch our attention was the disproportion among them. While we don't want to make broad generalizations about all teenagers based on our small interview sample size of twenty-seven, these findings do raise interesting questions about how teenagers talk about faith today.

Behavior

The category of "behavior" included acting out faith and living Christian morals. Teenagers talked about "acting Christian," "living differently," "being an example," "helping others," "loving others" as well as practices such as going to church and reading the Bible. Here are a few excerpts to give you a sense for students' own wording:

> What it means to be a Christian is doing what God tells you. To be obedient to God, to follow in the way of Jesus Christ. We are called Christians for a reason—to really follow what Jesus Christ told us to do, and then to follow him. We can't be Jesus, we will never be him, but we can have his morals. Just following the Word and all that, and also evangelizing and being kind to anyone.
>
> Daniel

> To live by God. Basically, to try your best to live the way that he lived, which is not easy—it's extremely difficult—but as long as you are doing your best to serve his kingdom with whatever gifts he has given you, that will naturally bring others to God through you, so you want to evangelize and bring others to God too.
>
> Hannah

Oh, that's an easy one. What does it mean for me to be a Christian in *my* eyes? Being a loving person to everyone around you. That is how I see it. I would point out a Christian in public as the person who is the most loving to everybody.

Leo

Behavior-oriented responses were by far the largest theme across the answers. Two thirds of interviewees noted behavior.

Belief

Responses identified as "belief" included this word and synonyms like "accepting Christ" and "having faith."[2] A few examples include the following:

I guess it means to be a firm believer in God.

Simone

I believe that Jesus saved us all and that accepting him will get you a life in heaven with him, so that is the most important thing.

Nick

I feel like it means someone—well, obviously someone who believes it—like, Jesus rose from the dead and is coming back. I feel like that is kind of the main point.

Hailey

Belief was the second most common theme, mentioned by about half of participants.

Relationship

Responses we identified as mostly about "relationship" included direct mentions of the word as well as experiences of love, relational qualities, or familial terms like "Father." Here are a couple of examples:

> I would say that being a Christian is having a relationship with the Lord . . . purely because he loves us.
>
> Rebekah

> Just being, like, a daughter of God.
>
> Claudia

Only one-quarter of interviewees mentioned relationship themes in their responses, and only one young person primarily described being a Christian in relational terms.

Other relational elements such as encountering God or a sense of transcendence were mostly absent. The Holy Spirit never showed up in teenagers' explanations of what it means to be a Christian. In fact, "spiritual" was mentioned only once.

What's more, young people talked in behavior-oriented terms nearly one-third more often than belief and over three times as much as relationship. In other words, *a teenager in our study was three times as likely to mention behavior over relationship* when talking about what it means to be a Christian.

Integrating Faith

If you're like us, you're probably both encouraged and discouraged by these responses. Faith includes being in relationship with God, believing, and actively living it out. But do young people have these elements in balance?

We did see some integration: one-third of students mentioned two of the three themes in their responses. *But only one young person integrated all three elements in his description of what it means to be a Christian.*

That teenager was Samuel, whom we met earlier in this chapter. He shared:

> Being a Christian is believing that Jesus died for you, and having a relationship with him, being able to create a bond with Jesus, to read God's Word; to just talk with someone. Knowing God and believing that he sent his Son to die for us. That's what being a Christian is. And living that out.

Now, no one wants their faith to be judged by their answer to a single question in the midst of a two-hour interview. So we don't want to read too much into these responses.

At the same time, we can think about this data like an off-the-cuff snapshot. And for many of the teenagers we interviewed, this snapshot looks a lot like "try-hard faith." While it's wonderful that young people put faith into action and see being a Christian as something they *do*, it's possible that belief and relationship sit on the sidelines.

Lack of faith integration was also a theme in our analysis of the responses of 2,092 young people to the 3 big questions of identity, belonging, and purpose. When looking at all the actual words teenagers shared in their responses, we found that religious terms (such as *church* and *God*) were hardly used at all—in only 6–7 percent of words for identity, 10–12 percent for belonging, and 2–3 percent for purpose.

We hope for a more holistic vision of what it means to follow Jesus. We bet you do too. You long for young people to know and live a robust picture of discipleship. You also wonder how to help them get there. The good news is that you can be part of the journey through stronger conversations and connections.

But first, we need to clarify what we mean by discipleship. If young people can't articulate it, there's a good chance the adults in their lives don't have an easy and repeatable way to do so.

Discipleship Is Our Everyday "Yes" to Jesus

If you're reading this book, you want to help teenagers move from their current answers to Christ-centered answers. How do we get there?

Discipleship is the bridge. *Discipleship is our everyday "Yes" to Jesus.*

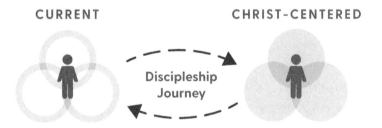

When we say that discipleship—our everyday "Yes" to Jesus—is a bridge from teenagers' current answers to Christ-centered answers, we envision it like this diagram. The young person stands in the intersection of the three interlocking domains of identity, belonging, and purpose. Their current answers, represented by the empty circles on the left, often represent less than the abundant life God offers. The Christ-centered answers, represented by the shaded circles on the right, embody the fruit of discipleship. In between the two, the discipleship bridge is marked by dotted arrows indicating that the discipleship journey is an ongoing, reciprocal process. Discipleship isn't just one way, and it isn't always a linear journey. Sometimes we take one or two (or three or forty-three) steps away from Christ's best answers for us. That's why faithful guides like you are so important!

In the Gospels, we see Jesus encounter all kinds of people and extend all kinds of invitations. But perhaps the most alarming and poignant is when he looks someone in the eye and offers, "Come, follow me."[3] The stakes are high. The ask is big.

Answering *yes* changes everything.

While we're not arguing the finer points of how salvation "works" here, it seems to us that Jesus' invitation to discipleship looks like an active and ongoing response to what God is doing in, around, and through us. So we propose that discipleship is an *everyday* "Yes."

What do we mean by that?

It's One Big Yes Followed by a Thousand Yeses

It's been wisely said that when we follow Jesus, we say "one big yes" followed by a thousand little yeses each day. Discipleship is a journey, a long pilgrimage, grounded in the stuff of normal life. It's holistic, embodied, and concrete. God's first word to us is "Yes,"[4] and in response, our yes is to look toward God and ask, "What today?" Today's yeses could look like reaching out to a hurting friend, seeking God through reflective prayer, or connecting with other disciples.

Our daily discipleship is a combination of the power of God at work to transform us and our "working out" our stories through what we do, say, and believe. It's about who we are and who we are becoming.[5] Discipleship, then, is also about growing in character and virtue. We can think of character like a well-worn pathway between who we say we are and what we actually do.[6]

So instead of a form of discipleship reduced to only behavior, belief, or relationship, as teenagers may see it, we can invite them into a more robust *way of life* based in trust. A yes—today, tomorrow, and every day after.

It's Not Just about Me but about Us

We do not follow Jesus in isolation. Discipleship is at once personal and shared; it's never only about "me" but always implies "us" at the family, church, community, society, and global levels—it's *our* everyday "Yes." Being a disciple means I belong with God's people.

Discipleship acknowledges that loving God means loving others,[7] even when it's hard. It involves knowing I am "saved by grace" while also knowing that what I do—and what we do together—matters because it impacts other people, who are all beloved image bearers of God. By the power of the Spirit, we open ourselves to see what Jesus sees and become neighbors the world needs—neighbors who enact justice and love mercy.[8]

We practice discipleship together because it's one of the ways we are like God: utterly relational. God is Father, Son, and Holy Spirit in mutual self-giving relationship. We are made in God's image, invited to participate in God's life, transformed by God's love, and sent out in God's power to love the world.

It's Both a Yes and a No

Jesus also offered stark terms for those who would walk with him: "Whoever does not carry their cross and follow me cannot be my disciple."[9]

Discipleship is a yes that requires a no. Following in the way of Jesus means we renounce other paths, allegiances, lords, and idols. This is discipleship's cost.[10]

What Do We Mean by "Christ-Centered Answers"?

When we talk about "Christ-centered answers" or "Jesus' better answers" throughout this book, we mean identity, belonging, and purpose oriented around Jesus. You can call them God-centered, Jesus-shaped, Spirit-filled, Christ-loving, or whatever phrase works for you and your tradition.

Our goal in this process was to determine what we would want a young person to internalize about their identity, belonging, and purpose that is most faithful to the story of God as revealed through the person of Jesus Christ and the Scriptures. Like the language we use to describe teenagers' current answers to the 3 big questions, the phrases describing Christ-centered answers also went through an extensive process of research, collaboration, and review—including with dozens of diverse teenagers who helped improve our wording.

We realize that sometimes the church falls into the temptation of making Jesus in our own image, resulting in more of a church-centered or self-centered than Christ-centered gospel.[a] When we talk about Christ-centered answers in this book, we *don't* mean partisan answers, sexist answers, racist answers, or ethnocentric answers. We mean reading the stories of Jesus alongside the cries of today's young people to answer their 3 big questions of identity, belonging, and purpose. Our deep hope, and what we've seen ourselves, is that this way of exploring the questions resonates as truly good news for teenagers.

a. See C. S. Song, *The Believing Heart: An Invitation to Story Theology* (Minneapolis: Fortress, 1999); and James H. Cone, *God of the Oppressed* (Maryknoll, NY: Orbis Books, 1997). Song suggests "Jesus-oriented" as a preferred term.

Sometimes that no means turning away from false answers to the 3 big questions of identity, belonging, and purpose and toward Christ-centered ones that free us to truly live.

It's Saying Yes and Then Inviting Others to Say Yes Too

Our response to Jesus is contagious. We become ambassadors who bring this story of good news to the poor, the rich, the hopeless, the forgotten, and the people with whom we share our everyday lives. We're always looking to expand the circle, to make room at the table.

The Church Puts Flesh on Better Answers

At the start of this chapter, we met Samuel. Samuel is deeply embedded in his church family. He has had the same mentor for the past four years who meets with him regularly and really helped him through the faith and friendship crises of his sophomore year. Samuel describes his mentor as "on call whenever. He has really pushed me in the right direction; if I ever need help, he is always trying to show me the way. Not so much push me—being able to let me experience it on my own, but also guide me. So he has been a really great influence."

This consistent adult has encouraged, challenged, and lived out faith for Samuel. But he's not the only one. Samuel has also had his youth pastor, his parents, his pastor, his peers and volunteer leaders in youth group, his extended family, and those who are like extended family.

In other words, Samuel has been surrounded by *the church*.

The church plays a unique—and increasingly rare—role in our culture. It is a community bound by collective beliefs and commitments that puts flesh on the message of Jesus through its shared life.

Sometimes that embodied faith is shown in the quiet example of the elder who shows up to shovel snow in the church parking lot week after week through the long winter. Or in the college student who faithfully drops off weekly groceries to an older shut-in during a quarantine. Or in a thousand other examples of on-the-ground faith in action— discipleship made concrete.

Other times the church puts flesh on better answers by telling stories. It repeats stories from the Bible as well as testimonies of saints through the ages and saints down the row in our worship services.

My (Brad's) youth ministry regularly invites adults in our church to share testimonies with our youth group. We ask them to think of a story about their own experience with God—either something recent or from when they were a teenager—and, if possible, to link it to one of the 3 big questions of identity, belonging, or purpose. Recently, we heard from a young adult about how he found joy in a new job among people experiencing homelessness, and from one of our pastors who shared openly about her long struggle with depression.

Students often tell us these testimonies are the highlights of our gatherings. The stories offer glimpses into what faith is like for real-life disciples beyond Sundays or what it was like for them as teenagers. The practice gives our students access to adults' not-put-together selves and to how they have wrestled with questions of faith.

Hearing faith stories builds faith language. Reflecting on our interviews with teenagers, teammate Jennifer Guerra

Aldana noted that sometimes the answers young people gave us felt like "borrowed language." She reflected, "I surely resonated with that—as a young person I borrowed a lot of language about my faith from the adults around me. Later I realized I had to sift through that language and figure out what language fit me best now as a young adult. So when I think of discipleship for young people, I think, let's inundate them with stories so they will have many to draw from."

What Any Adult Can Do as a Starting Point

As we think about how the church can be present with teenagers and give them a big bank of "borrowed" stories and language to scaffold their faith, we might like the idea in theory but get stuck in practice. We spend time with teenagers, but we don't know what to do to shape their journey toward Jesus-filled identity, belonging, and purpose.

As a Young Life leader in college, I (Kara) knew I was supposed to have some sort of "spiritual" conversation with teenagers when I met with them. So I set a goal to bring up God at least once every time I took a student out for frozen yogurt (frozen yogurt was all the rage when I was in college). I even had a strategy for *when* to bring up God. It needed to be far enough in the conversation that I had already bonded with the student but not one of the last questions I raised. So I'd usually shoot for talking about God—once—about two-thirds of the way into the conversation.

I was well-intentioned, but talking about God was an add-on—a forced three-minute interruption that didn't even shape our conversation, let alone that young person's faith.

It was sort of like walking students partway across the discipleship bridge, then shuffling back before anything got too serious.

What does it look like to be a faithful guide on that path? Picking up on the practice of sharing our testimonies and lives, here are three steps we can take with young people to create better conversations.[11]

NOW

First, we *listen for what is going on NOW in students' identity, belonging, and purpose.*

As we explored in chapter 2, listening opens the door for empathy. When we're with a young person, we can start by considering what's going on right now in their quest for answers.

Sometimes the "now" is right on the surface: a friend group falls apart, college applications are almost due, she gets cut from the team, he discovers a love for theater. When we're present in these moments, we hear a teenager processing one or more of the big questions out loud.

Other times the answer is less obvious. We may get the put-together version of the story or the closed-door answers of "fine" or "good." As we ask more questions and do more exploring, we can listen for the answers below the water—sometimes *way* below.

GOD

Next, we practice wondering and discernment. This puts us in a posture to *look for how GOD is present with students* and then *explore better Christ-centered answers* to their 3 big questions.

In this part of the conversation, we gain perspective in order to talk about the "now" concerns in light of God's nature, promises, presence, and action. We do this by wondering how God's Spirit is already in the midst of the current situation and inviting the student to see it. As adult mentors, leaders, or parents, we can help a young person discern the ways God is active. We may use specific prompts and questions such as these:

> I wonder how God might be at work through this situation? or, I wonder what God is up to here?
>
> I wonder if you've sensed God's Spirit present with you in this?
>
> How can I help you pray about this?

Together, we can explore the Christ-centered answers that free a young person to live out of a truer sense of identity, belonging, and purpose.

HOW

Eventually, we can offer direction. The *HOW* part of the conversation *helps a teenager take a next step toward living out better answers.* But be careful not to jump into this mode

One helpful practice for those of us adults who love to jump in with advice is to internally ask ourselves, Why am I talking? before we start dispensing our wisdom. You can memorize this question with a helpful acronym: WAIT (Why Am I Talking?).[a] Then remind yourself to refocus on where you are in the conversation: NOW, GOD, or HOW.

a. The origin of this widely used acronym is difficult to nail down, but it has been popularized by The Empowerment Dynamic. David Emerald and Robert Lanphear, *The Power of TED* (*The Empowerment Dynamic): 10th Anniversary Edition* (Edinburgh, Scotland: Polaris Publishing, 2015); and David Emerald, *Power of TED*, 2020, https://poweroftted.com/w-a-i-t-why-am-i-talking-2/.

too soon. We become a trusted guide only *after* we have listened well and empathized. At that point, we can practice truth telling, leading them into more faithful discipleship.

This NOW-GOD-HOW conversation framework gives us the skills we need to help teenagers move toward transformation. The rest of this book offers ideas and tools to help you put it into action.

One Adult Can Be the Bridge

When I (Brad) was a high school junior and new to following Jesus, Gaylene was one of our church's youth leaders. Gaylene was a single mom who showed me better answers to the big questions because she not only taught the Bible to our small high school group but also lived out better answers herself.

I knew her testimony of leaving an emotionally abusive marriage for the sake of her teenaged daughters. I witnessed her courage to keep them connected in a church community, driving them to midweek youth group after a long day at work or taking a Friday off to help lead a retreat. The one Bible study I still remember her leading was on the Beatitudes in Matthew 5 because she was someone who so obviously embodied them.

You don't have to be as courageous or devoted as Gaylene to make a difference. But whatever your situation, the young people in your life need *you* to be the bridge to better answers to their 3 big questions. As a caring adult who lives out their life and faith alongside a young person, you can make a deep impact in their adolescent years—and throughout their lifetime.

Up to this point in the book, we've met today's generation, considered how to listen for and empathize with their 3 big questions, and explored discipleship as the pathway to Christ-centered answers. The following chapters offer more specific ideas to help you be a bridge to better answers and over three hundred questions you can ask any teenager.

First, we turn our attention to identity, the question *Who am I?*

REFLECT and APPLY

1. How have you seen faith play out among behavior, belief, and relationship in your own life—especially in your teenage years?

2. What do you see in the teenagers you know when it comes to these elements of being a Christian? Which of the three do you think they lean toward most?

3. How do you talk about discipleship with young people? What resonates with you about our description of discipleship as our everyday "Yes" to Jesus? What would you change?

4. How have you been shaped by the testimonies of other Jesus followers? How does your ministry or family make space for young people to hear stories of transformation and real-life faithfulness?

5. Think about a recent conversation with a teenager. How could the NOW-GOD-HOW framework have been helpful in the moment?

PART II

WHO
AM I?

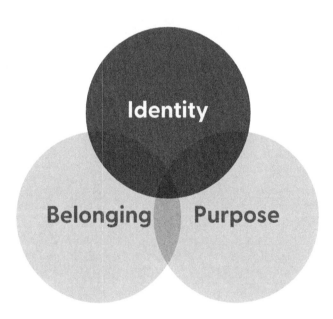

The Big Question
of Identity

I think a lot about what other people think of me ... whether or not somebody likes me. Whether they thought what I said was weird or stuff like that. I envy the people who are like, "I don't really care." I wish that was me, but it's not.

Sue

Of any play or musical I (Kara) have ever seen, *Dear Evan Hansen* drew the youngest crowd.

In front of the five Powells sat two families with kids ranging from middle school to college. Behind us sat a half row of talkative twentysomethings. As I swiveled to survey the rest of the audience, I saw few over sixty.

The show, known for its authentic exploration of teen anxiety, opens with a spotlight shining on seventeen-year-old Evan Hansen, sitting on his bed, staring at a letter to himself.

Dear Evan Hansen, today is going to be an amazing day, and here's why.

> Because today, all you have to do is just be yourself.
> *(Beat.)*
> But also confident. That's important. And interesting.
> Easy to talk to. Approachable. But mostly be yourself. That's
> the big, that's number one. Be yourself. Be true to yourself.[1]

In ten short sentences, Evan gives himself the advice to "be yourself" four times. One of those times he adds a small but critical word: *just*.

As leaders, mentors, and parents, we add "just" to our advice when what we're asking for seems relatively simple and straightforward. At least to us.

"*Just* make sure to register for camp before the deadline."

"*Just* get the information from the website."

"*Just* take ten minutes and clean up your room."

And of course, "*Just* be yourself."

Those of us over twenty-five likely find it easier to *just* be ourselves. In general, we'd rather play the personality cards in our hand than grab new cards from the deck and act like someone we're not. But teenagers are still figuring out which identity cards to keep and which to discard. The admonition to "(just) be yourself" raises the stakes, leaving them wondering if they'll eventually have to fold.

Lilly, an Asian American twelfth grader we interviewed, feels the tension between the cards that define her at school and those that define her at church. She describes herself at school as more "laid back," while at church, she's more "conservative."

Since friends from both school and church follow her on social media, Lilly confessed during our interviews, "I don't know how to combine these two personalities into one social media account. I don't know what or when to post." It's almost like she's playing two entirely different hands at the same time—with two different groups.

As a result, she hardly ever posts anything about herself. She can't navigate both audiences simultaneously, so it's easier not to try.

While many of her friends' Instagram bios describe themselves, Lilly opted to put nothing on her own. Simply her name.

For Lilly, no description is better than one that pigeonholes her. Or worse still, one that might repel a friend group, a fate Lilly tries to avoid at all costs.

Defining Identity: Who Am I?

Our identity is *our view of ourselves*. All too often teenagers like Lilly find that being "themselves" feels inches—or sometimes miles—beyond their reach. In part, this is because being yourself is too low of a bar. They seek a loftier goal; they want to be their "*best* selves."[2]

In addition, often a teenager's self (best or otherwise) is actually a mixture of several selves. While being "yourself" implies a singular self, the average teenager is constantly shuffling through multiple identities—trying to figure out which of their "selves" to play at that moment. Who they are in the neighborhood or at home is different from who they are at school or at their after-school job.

All those are different from who they are at church.

Furthermore, "being yourself" is tricky because young people are rarely the sole source of their identities. The identity of Lilly and every teenager you know is partly formed by the collective influence of family members, friends, and other adult authority figures.

Four Current Answers for Identity: I Am . . .

In essence, a teenager's identity is the word or phrase they use to finish this sentence: "I am _____."

Given what we heard from Lilly and others, as well as our review of both academic studies and popular sources, we think US teenagers tend to finish that sentence with one of four phrases.[3]

I Am What Others Expect

> I am what others want or need me to be. I constantly feel pressure to live up to the expectations of family, teachers, friends, church, and society.

Whether we're thirteen, forty-three, or seventy-three years old, it's inevitable that our view of ourselves is shaped by others. According to our friend and practical theologian Andy Root, "No identity is discovered in a vacuum; we cannot truly find ourselves without finding ourselves with someone."[4]

But for teenage identity development, others' influence is on steroids. In fact, this first answer was the most common source of identity in the students we interviewed.

Imagine every teenager's day is like a play performed before a packed audience. On the far right of the theater sits their nuclear family, surrounded by extended family members. The center of the audience is full of friends from school, work, sports, their neighborhood, and other extracurricular activities.

Just to the left of these diverse friends are members of their church. Next to church members sit several rows of teachers, coaches, and mentors.

In the front row are those they follow on social media, with other cultural messengers about success, beauty, and achievement perched in the balcony.

The teenager's task: to try to please every audience member. At every moment. It's exhausting to switch from being the family jokester at home to the obedient academic at school to the faith-filled youth group superstar at church.

The majority of teenagers try their best to please one audience at a time. When they are at school, they use the lines and choreography that appease their school friends and teachers. At home, church, and in their neighborhood, they swap scripts.

Sometimes a young person is aware of and can articulate the various crowds they try to please. Rebekah, a White twelfth grader from the South, chronicled her earlier teenage years when "I just really, really, *really* cared about what other people thought about me. And I *really* wanted to have the right friends and do the right things."

Rebekah pointed her finger at a handful of imaginary people: "I was whatever I wanted to be for you, and for you, and for you. I didn't have any stability. I kept looking for satisfaction, but none of it was working."

In our interviews, immigrants and teenagers from diverse ethnic environments often felt amplified pressure to

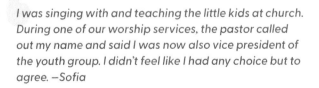

I was singing with and teaching the little kids at church. During one of our worship services, the pastor called out my name and said I was now also vice president of the youth group. I didn't feel like I had any choice but to agree. —Sofia

> My AP teachers have seen how I work and expect that I
> do well on exams. I think they grade me a little bit harder,
> and I guess that pressures me because sometimes I get
> lower grades than other people. That kind of stresses me
> out. −Arthur

please multiple audiences. Claudia, a Latina getting ready
to graduate from high school on the West Coast, used the
word "breakdown" to describe an experience from her junior
year to Kat Armas, her interviewer. Switching back and forth
between the two prominent ethnicities within her clusters
of friends became overwhelmingly stressful. She shared with
Kat a memory of tearfully telling a teacher, "It is really tiring
going between my Latino and Korean friends at school. It's
just *so* exhausting."[5]

Similarly, faith-centered teenagers feel the stress of pleasing
voices both inside and outside their church. Part of why Lilly refused to define herself in her social media biography is because
of the social and political stances assumed about Christians.
Lilly's school friends presume that since she's "religious," she's
"obviously going to be conservative or Republican." But Lilly
describes herself as "politically pro-choice but personally pro-
life," a position that is an internal strain for Lilly but "plays well
with my non-Christian friends." This tension leaves Lilly in an
internal and external tug-of-war, with different friend groups
pulling to shape her self-definition after their own.

I Am Not _____ Enough

> I fill in the blank with whatever I feel most judged about by oth-
> ers or myself: funny, smart, athletic, thin, pretty, accomplished,
> Black/Latino/Asian, and so on.

Feeling inadequate or "not enough" was mentioned overtly by about three-fourths of the high school students we interviewed. When it wasn't mentioned explicitly, it was a frequent identity subtext. They don't feel:

- smart enough
- pretty enough
- strong enough
- popular enough
- accomplished enough
- perfect enough

Lilly plummets emotionally when she makes a mistake. Mistakes "bum me out for like the whole day. I know it is human to make mistakes. But it just makes *me* feel really bad."

Natalie, a ninth grader on the East Coast, doesn't feel thin enough—unless she's wearing the right pair of jeans. When asked when she feels best about herself, Natalie confided, "This is going to sound silly, but I have a favorite pair of jeans that flatter me the most. Every single time I wear them, people are like, 'Wow, did you get skinnier?' I'm like, 'No, it's just the jeans.' I can walk around confidently in those jeans."

When it comes to not feeling "enough," immigrant and young people of color often experience an additional layer of complexity. Simone remembers painful elementary school moments when she was made fun of by other Black students for being too dark skinned, a prejudice frequently referred to as "colorism."

Daniel, a biracial Asian and African American eleventh grader, feels the sting of ethnic-identity stereotypes on the

Colorism is a by-product of generations of racialized hierarchy. It's an experience of being judged by skin tone and happens across racial groups as well as within them.[a] In one study of African American adolescents, 92 percent reported they liked their skin color. However, around one-third of those same respondents would prefer lighter skin if given the choice.[b]

basketball court. He doesn't use the same slang as some of the other Black players, so he feels "separated" and "not included" by his teammates. They say he's not "Black enough" in his way of speaking.

Student by student, the specific adjective differs but the feeling of not measuring up is nearly universal.

I Am My Image

I curate the identity I want the world to see through social media and beyond. I'm working on the brand—or style—I want to project. Sometimes it's more like a mask I wear.

Whether it's the difference between Nike and Under Armour, or Diet Coke and Diet Pepsi, a brand is what makes one product, or one person, different from another. It's what sets you apart. It's what makes you, you.

And it's important to teenagers.

a. Colorism is a form of cultural racism, which "refers to representations, messages and stories conveying the idea that behaviors and values associated with white people or 'whiteness' are automatically 'better' or more 'normal' than those associated with other racially defined groups.... Cultural racism is also a powerful force in maintaining systems of internalized supremacy and internalized racism. It does that by influencing collective beliefs about what constitutes appropriate behavior, what is seen as beautiful, and the value placed on various forms of expression." Sally Leiderman, Maggie Potapchuk, and Shakti Butler, "Cultural Racism," Racial Equity Tools, accessed July 16, 2020, https://www.racialequitytools.org/glossary. For a helpful resource for teachers and other adults working with teenagers, see David Knight, "What's Colorism?," *Teaching Tolerance* 51 (Fall 2015), https://www.tolerance.org/magazine/fall-2015/whats-colorism.

b. Tracy L. Robinson and Janie V. Ward, "African American Adolescents and Skin Color," *Journal of Black Psychology* 21, no. 3 (1995): 264, as cited in Elizabeth A. Adams, Beth E. Kurtz-Costes, and Adam J. Hoffman, "Skin Tone Bias among African Americans: Antecedents and Consequences across the Life Span," *Developmental Review* 40 (June 2016): 93–116, https://doi.org/10.1016/j.dr.2016.03.002.

Especially in this era of heavy social media use, many teenagers think about—and feel pressure to work on—their brand.[6] The only extracurricular hobby shared by all students we interviewed was social media. Not everyone we interviewed did their homework every day, but everyone was daily viewing, sharing, and liking.

While teenagers certainly have cared about image in the past, our social media age affords young people unique access to the technology that allows them to in essence *advertise* themselves. Consequently, marketing expert Sarah Weise concludes that today's young people are "intuitively segmenting and curating personal brands."[7]

Teenagers believe that with the right brand identity, anyone (including them) can become "internet famous."

And every moment is a broadcast opportunity. Even when it maybe shouldn't be.

That's how many of these teenagers have been treated by their parents since they were born. Kids' parents and guardians were on social media posting their quips and mistakes, awards and injuries, all before they could choose the moment or edit the look. No wonder they feel the desire to self-curate today.

Natalie didn't want to tell our interviewer how much she was on Instagram daily. While she wouldn't give him a specific number of hours, she admitted it surpassed five hours per day and that she spent more time each day on social media than sleeping.

When asked which parts of her identity she divulges and which she hides, Natalie was quick to say that she shows her "funny side." She described, "If you look at my story or the captions on my post, it's always a joke. I'm always laughing about something."

Natalie was one of a host of students we interviewed who characterized themselves—and wanted others to think of them—as "fun" or "funny." Other common self-descriptors used were "nice" and "chill." What we heard in our interviews was echoed in a linguistic analysis of 2,092 youth group students. Over three-quarters of students responded to some version of the question "Who am I?" using words associated with positive emotion—words like "funny," "nice," "kind," and "friendly." Don't be surprised if students' initial self-descriptions are as common and lighthearted as these. Just keep listening for what's beyond the veil of image management.

In her effort to appear fun and funny, Natalie never admits on social media when she's miserable. At most, she will post something like, "Man, I wish I had a coffee right now" with a "little sad face emoji," but she doesn't share any more than that.

Unless she can make a joke out of her gloom. She remembered recently when "someone knocked into me and I fell. After that, I definitely posted, 'Y'all, I literally just fell in front of everyone.'"

That calamity fit Natalie's fun and funny brand, so it made the cut.

I Am More Than My Label

I am more than what others say about me, including my mental health or learning-style diagnoses, stereotypes about my race or ethnicity, my test scores, or my past trauma.

Millennials have certainly received (more than!) their share of negative labels. Born between 1980 and 2000, the millennial generation has been tagged "lazy," "entitled," and "narcissistic."[8]

The generation of teenagers currently in front of us is postmillennial, and they are often known as either iGen or Gen Z. The descriptors we shared in chapter 1 of anxious, adaptive, and diverse thus far seem more favorable than those for millennials (at least two out of the three).

Yet even if a label is positive, it's still a generalization. Today's teenagers want to be known for more than their label. Especially when—as is the case with broad descriptions about their generation—the label is imposed on them. Gen Z expert Joi Freeman describes this way of interacting with identity using the metaphor of a bouquet. "Whereas recent generations may have seen identity options like various colors of roses in one bouquet, Gen Z tends to look at identity like an assortment of many types of flowers bundled together—a collection of experiences. I can be a banker and an artist. It doesn't have to look congruent. Identity isn't just one thing—all of these pieces make up who I am."[9]

Simone felt like, while her identity was in flux, what was most important was that *she be the one* to define herself. She asserted confidently, "I truly despise going with trends. I like people being themselves. If I'm around a group of people who I feel are *the* same person or are copying each other, I go out of my way not to copy them. If they're all wearing black, I'll wear red, yellow, pink, blue. I like to be my own person."

Researchers call this sense of self-determination "agency," meaning the freedom (and often privilege) to direct your actions toward a specific purpose. When it comes to defining who they are, some students feel they have as much agency as Simone. Unfortunately, many lack that sense of agency and end up subject to others' whims and preferences.

We recognize that questions about LGBTQ identity are both prominent and controversial within many churches and traditions. Our purpose in placing the spotlight on LGBTQ teenagers is not to take a theological position about human sexuality but rather to urge you as a caring adult to listen and empathize. Young people who identify as LGBTQ face particular challenges and struggles as well as unique affirmation and validation.

Mental health concerns are paramount for LGBTQ teenagers, often related to the stereotyping, discrimination, and bullying they experience as a result of living with this label. They seriously contemplate suicide at almost three times the rate of non-LGBTQ teens and are almost five times as likely to have attempted suicide. What's more, LGBTQ-identifying young people who experience family rejection are over eight times as likely to have attempted suicide as LGBTQ peers who report no or low levels of family rejection.[a] Regardless of your convictions, we hope you invite any LGBTQ-identifying young people in your life to share more about their journey and what they most need from caring adults.

Our experience with students who identify as LGBTQ aligns with research findings that queer youth find it distressing to conceal that part of their identity on social media.[10] Yet their gay identity wasn't their only defining feature. As one young person in a focus group clearly stated, "I'm part of the LGBT Alliance club at my school. And what I hear often from other teens is, 'Yes, I'm LGBT, and even though it's my identity, it doesn't mean it's the only thing or most important thing about me. I am also _____. But people tend to put you in a box and only think of you a certain way once they get a certain label about you.'"

a. The statistics were compiled from various sources by the Trevor Project, a crisis intervention and suicide prevention resource for LGBTQ teenagers and those who support them. See https://www.thetrevorproject.org /resources/preventing-suicide/facts-about-suicide/. If you know a young person who needs help, they can call the Trevor Project hotline at 1-866-488-7386 or text START to 678-678.

Our interviewees also showed significant agency in pushing against ethnic and racial stereotypes. Kevin is a half-Black, half-Asian senior who describes his ethnic identity as "Blasian." His Asian relatives expect him to get all As in school, offering a family motto that he "should get As . . . because Asian starts with A."

While Kevin earns high grades at school, he rejects the prejudice that he should do so because he's a particular ethnicity. He has chosen a less prestigious college because its major aligns with his sense of God's call for his future. He knows his decision will distress his family and surprise some of his classmates, but he's glad to push against others' knee-jerk expectations due to his cultural background.

While Kevin sought to transcend identity assumptions based on his association with particular ethnic *groups*, others were determined to rise above identity labels tacked on to them as *individuals*. Often this was a student's quest to be viewed as more than their diagnosis. In our study, young people diagnosed with a mental health or physical challenge or as someone who learns differently seemed fairly comfortable talking about their diagnosis. But they also wanted to be viewed as more than someone who struggles with a particular challenge or who receives extra attention in class. Their diagnosis was an important slice of who they are, but there was so much more to them.

Based on our interviews, we place students' feelings of not being "White enough," "Black enough," or "Asian enough" in two current identity categories: "I am not _____ enough" and "I am more than my label." We've found that external or internal expectations about cultural or ethnic identity can be doubly complex for teenagers.

> I let people know I'm a Christian, and sometimes I get
> that look like it's kind of surprising that I am because they
> know Christians are judgmental and all that stuff. But I'm
> very welcoming and happy, very open-minded and ac-
> cepting of people. I feel like I have an obligation—not only
> for myself but for others—to show that being a Christian
> is not what they say, it is more of a community that loves
> one another no matter what; we are always there for
> you. —Gabriel

Janelle was fifteen minutes into her first interview when she volunteered information and then answered follow-up questions about the prescription medicine she takes for her generalized anxiety disorder. Later in the discussion, she freely explained how her ongoing journey with mental health had birthed her growing desire to study psychology and eventually become a therapist.

While Janelle talked openly about her mental health diagnosis, she also wanted to discuss the novels she devoured in her free time and her volunteer work in her church's children's ministry. Her anxiety was a label that fit, but she was more likely to define herself as a reader or as someone who loves serving elementary-aged children.

Since no agreed-upon definition exists for a "disability," it's difficult to accurately measure the prevalence of disabilities among teenagers. About one out of six children and teenagers has been diagnosed with a developmental disability of some kind, one in fifty-four specifically with Autism Spectrum Disorder.[a]

a. "Data & Statistics on Autism Spectrum Disorder," Centers for Disease Control and Prevention, June 16, 2020, https://www.cdc.gov/ncbddd/autism/data.html.

Common Misunderstandings about Teenage Anxiety

The mental health struggles discussed in chapter 1 were pervasive not only for Janelle but also for many of the students we interviewed. Rebekah battles anxiety if she's by herself for very long. "I get worried about what is happening at that moment. Or what's going to happen next. Once anxiety takes over, I can't focus on one thing at a time."

In ninth grade, Natalie's anxiety about school was so intense that she would feel ill and usually vomit daily around 2 a.m. or 7 a.m.

In chapter 5, we provide the tools you need to respond to young people suffering from stress and anxiety. But first we want to unpack what you and other mentors or parents might misunderstand about mental health.

Misunderstanding #1: Only Some Teenagers Have Anxiety

Not every teenager has psychologically diagnosable anxiety, but more do than you might guess. As a reminder from chapter 1, one-third of the US population is affected by an anxiety disorder during their lifetime.[a] One-half of adolescents are growing up below the poverty line or in low-income homes, which tends to increase the likelihood of mental health struggles.[b]

Almost every teenager feels stressed regularly. *In our interviews, every single student felt anxious at times, and typically far more often than they wished.*

Misunderstanding #2: Our Mental Health Issues Are Due to Technology

It is true that there was a definitive increase in mental health challenges in 2012, which is when the proportion of Americans owning smartphones surpassed 50 percent. And mental health concerns have continued to rise. The good news is that risk behaviors that generally involve two or more young people, such as sexual activity, substance use, and teen pregnancy, all dropped right around then. Risk behaviors experienced alone—often when you're seeing online what everyone is doing without you—are escalating.[c]

But we at FYI, along with other mental health researchers, don't think technology is the only culprit. Many of today's parenting styles contribute to teen anxiety. Parents often put pressure on kids to perform. Or parents swoop in to rescue kids instead of letting them work through their own challenges and develop resilience.

Furthermore, teenagers' busy schedules also increase stress and anxiety. Concerned about the effects of busyness on kids' mental health, well-respected adolescent researcher Lisa Damour recommends that 25 percent of a young person's schedule be unplanned and unscheduled to provide adequate margin.[d] That's a far cry from the all-day-rushing-from-activity-to-activity pace of today's teenagers who fear that any failure or missed opportunity equals a blown-up life.

The polar opposite of a busy schedule can also spark anxiety. In the first two months of the COVID-19 pandemic and the broad nationwide quarantine in spring 2020, mental health hotlines experienced a 40 percent jump in calls and texts—a majority from young people.[e] Suddenly isolated from their friends and forced to hole up at home in fear, teenagers were left feeling anxious and powerless.

Misunderstanding #3: Bringing Up Anxiety, Depression, or Suicidal Thoughts with a Teenager Makes It Worse

Young people are hearing about anxiety and suicide daily online and at school. Teachers may be trained and prepared to bring up related topics in class. In the state of California, recent legislation mandates middle schools and high schools include a suicide hotline number on the back of student ID cards.

Yet tragically, the same conversations aren't happening in most churches. Only 4 percent of churchgoers who have had a close friend or family member die by suicide report that church members or leaders were aware of their loved one's struggles.[f]

It's time to break the silence in the typical church and home. In the next chapter, we give you the conversation prompts and connections to do so.

Misunderstanding #4: When a Young Person Feels Anxious, We Have to Problem Solve with Them Immediately

We need to empathize and *listen immediately* to a stressed or anxious young person. In some (often more serious) cases, such as when there are self-harm or suicidal thoughts present, we need to intervene at that very moment to establish safety.

But many times young people may not be ready for problem solving yet. Damour uses the image of a glitter globe to explain her best strategy for problem solving. If the glitter is still swirling, meaning the teenager is still wound up emotionally, they aren't yet ready to brainstorm best solutions and next steps.

Damour's advice? First let the glitter settle. Avoid jumping in too soon with all-hands-on-deck reassurances or suggestions. Instead, let the young person's emotions calm down (at least a bit). Communicate your confidence that their panic will eventually subside, making problem solving more possible.[9]

If, upon the glitter settling, you realize that the young person's challenges are beyond your capacity to handle, you likely need to recommend a trained therapist. (See chapter 5 for practical ideas on finding a qualified mental health professional in your area.)

Big Question	Focus	Description	Current Answers
Who am I?	Identity	Our view of ourselves	*I am . . .* • what others expect. • not _____ enough. • my image. • more than my label.

a. Borwin Bandelow and Sophie Michaelis, "Epidemiology of Anxiety Disorders," *Dialogues in Clinical Neuroscience* 17, no. 3 (September 2015): 327–35.

b. Candice L. Odgers and Michael B. Robb, *Tweens, Teens, Tech, and Mental Health* (San Francisco: Common Sense Media, 2020), 19.

c. Jean M. Twenge, "Have Smartphones Destroyed a Generation?," *Atlantic*, September 2017, https://www.theatlantic.com/magazine/archive/2017/09/has-the-smartphone-destroyed-a-generation/534198/.

d. Lisa Damour, *Under Pressure* (New York: Ballantine Books, 2019), 61.

e. Andrea Petersen, "The Struggle to Cope with Depression Amid Coronavirus," *Wall Street Journal*, April 12, 2020, https://adaa.org/sites/default/files/WSJ%20Article%20-%20Depression%20-%20Charles%20Nemeroff%20April%2012%202020.pdf.

f. Bob Smietana, "1 in 3 Protestant Churchgoers Personally Affected by Suicide," *Christianity Today*, September 29, 2017, https://www.christianitytoday.com/news/2017/september/protestant-churches-pastors-views-on-suicide-aacc-liberty.html.

g. Damour, *Under Pressure*, 38–40.

Identity in Flux

It's quite likely that Lilly refused to define herself in her social media biography not only because of the multiple audiences watching (and judging) her but also because she doesn't yet know how to define herself.

Helen Jun, Lilly's interviewer, asked her, "In thinking about your identity, when you ask yourself, 'Who am I?' what sorts of words or phrases come to mind?"

Pausing, Lilly responded, "Um [long pause] I have no idea."

Trying to make Lilly comfortable with her uncertainty, Helen continued, "That is totally normal. Sometimes we don't think about those questions much. What sort of things come to mind when you think about how you understand yourself?"

Lilly laughed and repeated the answer she had given moments earlier: "Um . . . I have no idea!"

Whether your nearest teenager is balancing multiple identities like Lilly or trying to establish themselves as more than any label or external expectations, we believe their ultimate identity comes from embracing God's truths about them. As we'll see in the next chapter, staying tethered to God's descriptions of us is what frees us to truly *just be ourselves*.

REFLECT and APPLY

1. Below are the four current answers young people commonly use to define their identity. To help you empathize with today's teenagers, reflect on your own experience of being a teenager. Rank the answers on a scale of 1 to 4, giving a 1 to the answer that was most common for you and a 4 to the one you identified with least.

   - _____ "I am what others expect."
   - _____ "I am not _____ enough."
   - _____ "I am my image."
   - _____ "I am more than my label."

2. When you were younger, what audiences most shaped your view of yourself? What gave them so much influence?

3. In what ways did you feel tugged between two or more audiences?

4. Given the multiple crowds and contexts that surrounded you, when were you most likely to feel like an imposter?

5. In what settings did you most feel like yourself?

6. Now think about a young person you know and repeat the same process, placing a 1 next to their most common identity answer and a 4 next to their least common identity answer.

- _____ "I am what others expect."

- _____ "I am not _____ enough."

- _____ "I am my image."

- _____ "I am more than my label."

7. What adjectives would the young people you know use to describe themselves?

8. In what ways are young people you're closest to trying to juggle multiple scripts and expectations from multiple audiences?

9. When do your young people feel most stressed and anxious?

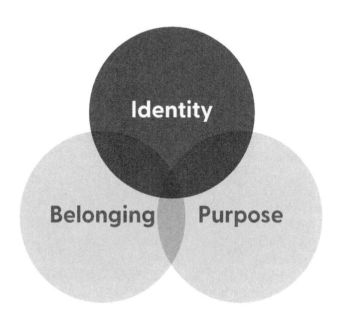

ENOUGH:
Jesus' Better Answer

I didn't really know who I was. And I didn't really care either. And I was like, "Wait, why isn't this working out?" And it wasn't until I realized, "Oh, that is a Jesus-sized hole I cannot fill on my own" that I knew who I was.

Rebekah

I think I have a unique point of view, growing up as a Christian and being queer. Am I really enough if I am not accepted for who I am? I do believe God loves me, and I feel I am enough. But sometimes it seems like other Christians don't believe that.

Dante[1]

God's transformation of our identity usually takes a lifetime. But sometimes the Holy Spirit changes it—and us—in an instant.

Just ask seventeen-year-old Sebastian.

Until two years ago, Sebastian's view of himself orbited around two powerful forces: friends and drugs. Recalling middle school and early high school during my (Kara's) first interview with him, Sebastian summarized, "Weed was a big part of my life."

Sebastian's dad was verbally (and occasionally physically) abusive, constantly berating him and redoing anything he tried to do around the house. Never feeling like he measured up at home, Sebastian gave up trying at school, and his grades subsequently plunged.

Most nights Sebastian came home around 2 a.m. after hanging out with friends. Often stoned and needing to unwind, he would turn on the TV and channel surf.

One early morning, he inexplicably flipped to a station playing Christian preaching that strangely hit home. Sebastian thought to himself, *I don't know why, but I feel really connected to this message. I need to change. I need Jesus.* Sitting alone in front of the glowing screen, Sebastian decided to follow Jesus and prayed the TV preacher's prayer.

Jesus' transformation of Sebastian's life was immediate. Before going to bed that night, Sebastian gathered all his marijuana and threw it in the trash.

In place of weed grew a fresh passion for Jesus' teachings and a new eagerness to serve at a local church. Googling to find churches nearby, Sebastian messaged one that seemed volunteer-friendly and received a response the next day. He's now been part of that church for two years.

His relationship with God and his church family has changed his identity. So much so that when I asked him to describe himself in our first interview, he used two words: "helper" and "giver."

Sebastian further unpacked his sense of himself: "Whether it's through physically lifting something heavy at church, or spiritually getting to sit and talk with someone and pray with them, I love to give back. Even at night, I don't put my phone on silent just in case a friend or someone from church needs to talk. I make sure people know that I will always help them."

Sebastian is currently a homeschool junior and a volunteer church intern, which he views as divine preparation for God's call to long-term vocational ministry. Every week as he works with a team to plan, set up, and lead his church's worship services and youth group, Sebastian gains a clearer sense of who he is and how the Holy Spirit wants to uniquely work through him to impact others.

The Christ-Centered Answer in One Word: ENOUGH

What was it that prompted Sebastian's 2 a.m. identity transformation from stoner to servant? What helps Sebastian and other teenagers let go of the lies that they should be defined by others, don't measure up, and are no more than their personal brand?

To answer those questions, our research team pored over Sebastian's and other students' interviews, seeking to understand the defining milestones in their identity journeys. In addition, we explored a host of Christ-centered messages that could be game changing in teenagers' search for answers to the big question of identity.

In the end, we landed on one theologically rich word that helps young people say a stronger everyday "Yes" to Jesus.

Enough.

Enough.

Enough.

In an era that fears and often expects scarcity, Jesus offers abundance. And through that abundance, *we're ENOUGH because of Jesus.*

We're ENOUGH Because of Jesus: John 6:1–15

While we have a front-row seat to Jesus' abundance throughout the Gospels, one passage in particular has helped me (Kara) rest my identity in God's ENOUGH-ness. Other than Jesus' resurrection, the miracle detailed in John 6:1–15 is the only miracle in all four Gospels.

The setting is springtime, shortly before the Passover, and having seen "the signs he had performed by healing the sick" (v. 2), a large crowd pursues Jesus near the Sea of Galilee. Concerned about the crowd's hunger, Jesus the healer now becomes Jesus the host.[2]

Bringing forward a young person with five (small) barley loaves and two (likely also small) fish, Andrew asks (perhaps somewhat sarcastically), "But how far will they go among so many?" (v. 9).[3]

But this disciple's lack of imagination doesn't stop Jesus from using the minuscule to feed the masses. Despite the meager available protein and carbs, Jesus gives thanks and starts distributing bread and fish to the ten to fifteen thousand gathered.[4]

Jesus offers not just a bite. Not merely a snack. But so much bread and fish that each crowd member receives "as much as they wanted" (v. 11).

Because We Are Made in God's Image, Jesus Declares Us ENOUGH

Jesus could have provided without working through what the disciples and young person scrounged up. He could have turned the nearest rocks into rolls. He could have converted the nearest foliage into fruit. Or he could have snapped his fingers (think Thanos in *Avengers: Infinity War*, but for

My faith hasn't just impacted my identity; it's shaped it completely. Regardless of what I do, my faith is the driving force in my life. —Arthur

nobler purposes) and presented a sumptuous Mediterranean meal of bread, cheese, and olives (anyone else getting hungry?).

But Jesus chooses to work through his followers. *Then and now, Jesus makes what we have, and who we are, ENOUGH.* He turns our not-enough into ENOUGH.

Our potential to change from not-enough to ENOUGH lies in our being created in God's image. We humans are the only part of creation made in the image of God, which instills in us a special potential relationship not just with God but with one another.

Just as our Triune God is a community of the Father, Son, and Holy Spirit, we best experience our ENOUGH-ness in community. Somewhat blind to God's potential flowing through us, we often realize that Jesus makes us ENOUGH as we draw out the best in one another. No one person on their own was sufficient in John 6; the young person *plus* Andrew (who introduced the young person to Jesus) *plus* the disciples who handed out food *plus* everyone who passed food to one another—all of these people together made the loaves and fish ENOUGH. As theologian and minister Marva Dawn highlights, "This sense of being made in God's image calls us all constantly to look for it in others and to do what we can to help them acknowledge it."[5] Together, we celebrate and call out the ENOUGH-ness Jesus offers.

Jesus Makes Us (More Than) ENOUGH

A child offering a handful of food to feed thousands feels like a joke. Parents would certainly post it on Facebook and label it #cute.

But Jesus takes the child seriously. Jesus makes the handful ENOUGH.

Actually, that's not quite right. *Jesus makes what we have, and who we are, more than ENOUGH.* Even after everyone had eaten their fill, the disciples loaded twelve baskets with leftover pieces of bread (John 6:13). They ended up with exponentially more than what they started with.

Jesus' ENOUGH-Ness Flows from Young People to All Generations

Here's more good news for teenagers across history: Jesus makes *what a young person offers* more than ENOUGH. Unlike the other three Gospels, which highlight kids regularly, John is otherwise absent of children. No baby Jesus, no twelve-year-old Jesus, no children healed, no kids in the center of conversation, and not a single other story about children.

Only one young person with some bread and small fish. We don't know from the text if it's a boy or a girl[6] or even their age, but we do know that Jesus works through them. In the presence of Jesus, this young person was affirmed as someone worthy of being there that day. Affirmed as a person with dignity and value. Affirmed as a tunnel through which the gifts of the Holy Spirit could reach others. Someone who was truly ENOUGH. It's just as true now as it was in the first century: *Jesus' generosity flows through a young person and spreads to all generations.*

Big Question	Focus	Description	Current Answers	Christ-Centered Answer
Who am I?	Identity	Our view of ourselves	*I am...* • what others expect. • not _____ enough. • my image. • more than my label.	I'm ENOUGH because of Jesus.

ENOUGH Gets Practical—Conversations and Connections

So after the crowd sees Jesus turn not-enough into ENOUGH, they understand perfectly who Jesus is and who that makes them, right?

Not even close.

Thanks to Jesus' miracle, they now view him as a prophet. The crowd intends to force him to be their king, not realizing that the path of Jesus' kingdom leads through the crucifixion.

Of course, Jesus' generosity and ENOUGH-ness raises an inevitable question: If Jesus makes what we have and who we are ENOUGH, why is there ever any lack—of food, money, love, or really anything? It's a good and fair question. And we can't give a definitive answer. Sometimes human sin—personal, collective, or systemic—blocks God's provision. Often circumstances out of human control (such as disease, natural disasters, and infertile land) interfere with God's ideal plan. At times, it's tough to even pinpoint the cause. Whatever the reason for the shortfall, often God overcomes that deficit by providing through others—just like in the first century when Jesus multiplied a young person's meal to feed the masses. In fact, in many cases the Holy Spirit uses the church to provide for those who are in need as a tangible witness to God's ENOUGH-ness.

If even the first-century followers who experienced Jesus in person failed to fully understand who Jesus was and what that meant for them, is it any wonder that we and our young people do the same today? Is it any surprise that we get trapped in the powerful vortex of the current flawed identity answers we discussed in the last chapter? Our failure to understand *who Jesus is* shortchanges our own search to discover the answer to the big question *Who am I?*

Since we believe expression deepens impression, we will give you two paths in this chapter's application of Jesus' better identity answer. (We'll do the same for belonging and purpose in chapters 7 and 9.)

First, we give you tools to have better *conversations* with young people so you can keep listening empathetically and help them say yes to Jesus' ENOUGH-ness.

During our season of interviews, one member of our research team was told by a close friend in youth ministry, "I cannot tell kids enough that God says they're ENOUGH." We agree, so this chapter provides you with a host of questions and statements that help you do just that.

In chapter 3, we introduced a three-step framework that you can use anytime to plunge into the deep end of conversational waters. We think NOW-GOD-HOW is such a good framework that we use it as a skeletal structure for every suggested discussion.

Second, we offer a few new action-oriented and relationship building *connections* for you to try with young people. In the case of identity, the connections we encourage will help both you and teenagers rest (metaphorically and literally) in God's ENOUGH-ness.

Some of these conversations and connections are a bit lengthy, so you may want to bring your book or ebook to your next teenage conversation or small group. Your teen-agers might tease you for having a book in hand, but that's often a good sign that they feel comfortable with you (at least that's what the two of us tell ourselves). Or if you want to be more covert, you can jot down a few notes or take a few pictures of the questions ahead of time. The more comfortable you get with this pattern, the less you'll need our prompts.

We've geared these conversations and connections to work for any adult who wants to disciple young people toward Jesus' better answers. Whether you are a ministry leader, mentor, parent, or other caring adult, you can draw from this toolbox to take your conversations and connections further and make them more fruitful. Because we've tested many of these ideas with actual ministries and families, at times we offer specific sidebar suggestions for those of us who are youth leaders or parents.

Conversations about Identity

A Conversation about Racial and Ethnic Identity

Depending on your background, you might be surprised by how often young people experience racial prejudice and racial inequity. According to one study, Black teenagers in the US experience an average of five instances of racial discrimination (individually, vicariously, online, or offline) daily.[7]

We don't know your ethnicity. Nor do we know the cultural background of the young people you care about most. But we agree with ministry leaders Brenda Salter McNeil and Rick Richardson:

Until we know who we are ethnically, we are unable to really reconcile genuinely with others. And until we know and recognize people for who they really are—including some of their history as a people—and then interact with them in ways that actually influence how we see ourselves, we cannot genuinely reconcile with them.[8]

The two of us find that we are changed when we go out of our way to listen, love, and learn from folks who are from social locations different from ours. We want to help you and young people talk about racial and cultural identity through the following conversation questions.

NOW

1. Can you share a specific example or story of how your race or ethnicity has shaped your life so far?

2. How would your parents' or grandparents' answers be different from yours?

3. How do you think your race and culture shape your view of yourself?

GOD

4. How does your race or ethnicity shape your faith or view of God?

HOW

5. What do you think your ethnicity or culture helps you understand well?

6. What might be some of your blind spots given your cultural background?

7. How can you compensate for, grow through, or overcome those blind spots?

Every day, I don't ever forget who I am. And I don't ever let anyone tell me who I am. —Jason

A Conversation to Unpack Identity Expectations

To help one or more teenagers understand how other voices shape their identity and how those expectations can clash, discuss these questions, some of which were lifted straight from our interviews (see the interview questions in full in appendix B).

NOW

1. When you ask yourself, "Who am I?" what sorts of words or phrases come to mind?
2. How would your friends describe you? If I asked one of them to tell me "Who is _____?" what do you think they would say?
3. What about your family—how would they describe you?
4. What do you think others might miss or get wrong about you?
5. Have you ever felt like you had to act a certain way because friends or your parents wanted you to? Can you please tell me more about that?
6. Have you ever felt you needed to be a certain way because of what people at church expected? Does a story come to mind about that?

GOD

7. How would you say your faith impacts your view of yourself?

For Leaders

When trying to help middle and high school students realize that their identity is more than the negative messages they hear from others, one urban youth pastor ended a talk by asking her students to repeat, "*I am who God says I am. I am important. My voice matters, and I am deeply loved.*"

They chanted those three sentences over and over as the Holy Spirit began to burn the truth that they are ENOUGH into their hearts and souls.

8. How do you wish your faith shaped your view of yourself?

   HOW

9. What would you have to do to elevate God's voice above the voices of others who are defining you?

10. What would you gain by doing so? What might you lose?

A Conversation about Who Makes You Feel (Not) ENOUGH

Whether it's people they *know*—like friends, family members, teachers, and pastors—or people they *know of*—like social media or YouTube celebrities—these discussion questions help teenagers think about which voices make them feel as if they don't measure up.

   NOW

1. On a scale of 1 to 5, with 1 being "really bad" and 5 being "really good," how do the following make you feel about yourself?

- your favorite teacher or coach
- your least favorite teacher or coach
- your mom/stepmom
- your dad/stepdad
- your brother/stepbrother
- your sister/stepsister
- your grandparents
- your boss, if you have one
- your pastor or youth pastor, if you have one
- others' social media posts about what they are up to
- friends you've grown distant from
- friends you're close to now
- your boyfriend or girlfriend, if you have one

2. Of all the people and things we've named, which ones make you feel like you're not enough?
3. I wonder how you could handle that person or voice differently than you are now?

GOD

4. Which of those people or things help you feel like God makes you ENOUGH?

HOW

5. What would you have to change in your life or schedule to get more time with them?
6. How can I support you as you think about making those changes?

For Families

As parents, stepparents, or caregivers, we're unaware of how our attempts to provide support annoy teenagers—unless we ask them. So occasionally I (Kara) ask my kids, "What could I do that would make it easier for you to talk with me about big stuff?"

Their most common responses? "Please stop asking so many questions." (It's ironic that that's their response to a question that I, in fact, just asked.)

As well as "Don't make a 'big thing' out of what we talk about." Our kids sometimes don't like it when I bring up insights we discussed about a movie last month or a vacation last year. I think it makes me seem too teacher-ish.

Do I still ask questions and sometimes bring up past experiences? You bet, but probably about half as much as I would if these weren't my kids' two pet peeves.

Conversations about ENOUGH Elsewhere in the Bible

To help you appreciate the full meaning of God making us ENOUGH, we encourage you and young people to explore the following Scripture passages on your own or together. Along with John 6:1–15, these passages can be compelling to meditate on, memorize, send by text, or compile into a small group or youth ministry teaching series.

- Genesis 1:1–31, especially verses 26–27: We are ENOUGH because we are made in God's image.
- Psalm 139:1–24, especially verse 14: Since we are fearfully and wonderfully made, we are ENOUGH.
- Matthew 5:13–16, especially verses 13–14: As God works through us, we are ENOUGH to be salt and light to our world.

- Mark 1:1–13, especially verse 11: As children of God, God views us as ENOUGH.
- Luke 7:36–50, especially verses 45–47: Even when others condemn us and we feel inadequate, God makes us ENOUGH.
- Romans 8:1–17, especially verse 1: No matter what we've done, God frees us from condemnation and makes us ENOUGH.
- 1 Corinthians 6:12–20, especially verse 19: God is ENOUGH to transform our bodies into temples, and together as the one temple of Christ, we are ENOUGH.
- 2 Corinthians 5:11–21, especially verse 17: Through Christ, we are new creations who are ENOUGH.
- Ephesians 2:1–10, especially verses 8–9: It's God's gift of grace, not our works, that makes us ENOUGH.
- 1 Peter 2:4–10, especially verses 9–10: As people chosen by God, we are ENOUGH.

Sabbath Connections about Identity

> Divine rest on the seventh day of creation has made clear that . . . YHWH is not a workaholic.
>
> Walter Brueggemann[9]

A cluttered schedule leads to a cluttered identity.

That's why Brad and I can think of no better historical Christian connection to help you and students say yes to Jesus' ENOUGH-ness than the Sabbath. Periodically, we need to push away the clutter and replace our impossibly

Talking A, B, C, D, E about Mental Health

Trapped in false answers to their 3 big questions of identity, belonging, and purpose and haunted by a pervasive sense of inadequacy and pressure, young people are riddled with stress. Given our desire to equip you and other caring adults, we curated the insights of some of our favorite mental health professionals into practical answers to four common questions about mental health.

How can I tell when a young person is dealing with greater-than-normal stress or anxiety?
In general, experts tell us to look out for the following:

- anything more intense or pronounced than usual for a young person (e.g., more or less sleeping or eating, mood swings)
- signs that they are having more trouble managing their emotions
- struggles dealing with the tasks of everyday life (like homework or chores)
- unhealthy coping strategies such as the use of alcohol, drugs, or self-harm

If you're worried, trust your gut and follow the steps in the next question.

Once I realize that a young person is dealing with a mental health struggle, what should I do?
We believe your best response can be summarized using the acronym **ABCDE.**

First, empathetically **ASK** the young person to rate their anxiety, stress, or depression on a scale of 1 to 10, with 10 being the worst. A rating of 1–3 is a normal level of anxiety we all experience from time to time, and a 4 or 5 is probably handleable. If they rate it a 6 or above, they probably need more help from you and likely also a trained professional.

Second, encourage the young person to **BREATHE** deeply. Have you ever noticed that when you get really stressed, your heart begins to beat faster? That's your heart's automatic gas pedal to accelerate oxygen to every extremity in emergencies. When you breathe deeply, your heart gets more oxygen and doesn't have to work as hard. As your heart slows down, your brain starts to get the message that you aren't in danger anymore. It's your body's simple, but powerful, brake pedal for out-of-control emotions like panic.

Third, help the young person **CENTER** on a core truth or phrase. What few words from a meaningful Scripture passage, worship song, or prayer could they repeat to themselves as a theological anchor? In my (Kara's) family, we've landed on "Emmanuel, God is with us" as a favorite mantra.

Fourth, help the young person **DEVELOP** a team. If they are likely to be anxious in their online math class or at their new job, help them think ahead of time about a friend or adult they could text or talk to in those moments. If you're not their parent, encourage them to let their parents know the depths of their stress.

As needed, invite them to consider seeing a professional therapist. The brain is an organ, and as with our heart and liver, the brain sometimes requires additional help to function properly. If you don't know a therapist you can recommend, contact a few churches or high schools for referrals or search for virtual teletherapy via services like betterhelp.com or talkspace.com.

Throughout your conversations, **EMPOWER** them to take future (often baby!) steps. One of my favorite phrases to simultaneously "feel with" young people while also emboldening them to move forward is "That stinks, and I think you can handle it."[a]

Is there a specific resource or hotline for young people who need immediate help?

The National Suicide Prevention Lifeline (1-800-273-TALK or suicide preventionlifeline.org) is a proven resource for young people in crisis as well as for concerned friends or family members.

In addition, the Steve Fund Crisis Text Line is an outstanding service dedicated to the mental health and emotional well-being of students of color that can be reached by texting STEVE to 741-741 or visiting stevefund.org/crisistextline.

Where can I get more ideas on how to help anxious young people?

At the Fuller Youth Institute, we've developed several Faith in an Anxious World resources, including a parent podcast series and a downloadable multimedia youth group curriculum. To find out more, visit fulleryouthinstitute.org/anxiousworld.

a. Lisa Damour, *Under Pressure* (New York: Ballantine Books, 2019), 45.

Another term for "connections" is *practices*. When we use the term *practices* in this book, we mean communally taught and historically rooted activities that embody an ultimate good. In addition to Sabbath, other common practices include worship, hospitality (see chapter 7), prayer, studying Scripture, testimony, confessing sin, witness, vocation, and working for justice (see chapter 9).

long to-do list with one discipleship goal: to Sabbath. For both of us as well as for many young people, reminders that we are ENOUGH and regular rhythms of Sabbath go hand in hand.

Derived from the Hebrew verb *shabbat*, or "rest from labor," the Sabbath mirrors God's own actions of working for six days and resting on the seventh (Gen. 2:2–3). In contrast to the relentless push to define ourselves by our abilities and accomplishments, a Sabbath offers identity-shaping disciplines[10] such as the following:

Silence, which is often uncomfortable but teaches us to wait, listen, and reconnect with God and ourselves.

Rest, which provides holistic rejuvenation and cultivates an acknowledgment of our limits and dependence upon God for ENOUGH.

Retreat, which is leaving our typical contexts and refraining from technology and other activities and spaces that often define us. We see Jesus model this when he leaves the crowd and withdraws with his disciples in John 6:3.

Worship, especially in weekly church gatherings with the people of God, which is arguably one of the most identity-forming practices of Christians today.

For Leaders

After practicing Sabbath more intentionally as a youth ministry for a couple of months, one Michigan youth pastor had the opportunity to preach about Sabbath to the entire congregation. Kyle included testimonies from high school students who shared about the work of preparing for a Sabbath, the challenge of practicing Sabbath in the midst of their busy lives, and what they had learned about themselves. By offering their experiences, these students were able to lead the entire church community forward in taking the time needed to know they were ENOUGH.

Connections to "Pray and Play"

We've been willing to work tirelessly on behalf of young people. But are we willing to rest on their behalf as well?

Nathan T. Stucky[11]

When I (Kara) first started practicing the Sabbath as a twentysomething, I was greatly helped by Eugene Peterson's description of Sabbath as a time to "pray and play."[12] For me, that meant extra time journaling and in a rejuvenating activity that was hard to squeeze into my other six days.

Invite your young people to make a list of all the ways this week or in the future they could "play" on a Sabbath (meaning do rejuvenating or fun activities by themselves or with others they don't normally have time for during the week).

Next, ask them to list what they could do to "pray" or get more focused time with God. (For most students, this list is tougher. If you're meeting with more than one student, feel free to encourage them to share their items aloud in hopes that it spurs more creativity.)

Ask students to circle the two or three items on each list that are most feasible or most appealing to try in the near future.

Discuss what they circled as well as what's left over.

1. What, if anything, do the items you circled have in common?
2. What prevents you from doing these circled items now?
3. During this upcoming week, when might you be able to make time for a Sabbath that incorporates one pray idea and one play idea?
4. Is there anything that I, or anyone else, could do to encourage you to have that Sabbath this week?
5. How would more time to pray and play help, or hinder, your sense that God has made you ENOUGH?

For Families

After connecting with her kids over Sabbath for a few weeks, one mom shared with her teenagers that she thought they had done a pretty good job resting as a family. After all, they had been preparing dinner together and working on a plan for their next summer's activities (two events that were squeezed out of a typical Sabbath-less week). The kids responded, "What are you talking about, Mom? We haven't been resting at all."

It turns out the mom's highly structured Sabbath plans were a far cry from what her teenagers craved. As a result of that conversation, the mom and kids now schedule a weekly family meeting in order to better structure their lives during the week, allowing their Sabbath to be freer and more spontaneous.

Sabbath Connections for Beginners

You might want to try the following starting points with one or more young people, cleverly referred to by one church in our training as "Sabblets."

1. One church boiled down the essence of the Sabbath to two questions: What will you say yes to on the Sabbath? And what will you say no to on the Sabbath? Offering students this simple yes/no dichotomy can help them name specific activities, patterns, and propensities they want to accept or avoid on their path to centering their identity in Jesus' ENOUGH-ness.

2. Another youth ministry focused on helping students identify the difference between *fruitful* work and rest (which advances our God-given identity, belonging, and purpose) and *unfruitful* work and rest (which has no ultimate objective and doesn't relieve our stress). Students were invited to track their work and rest—and whether it had been fruitful or unfruitful—every morning, afternoon, and evening.

3. A full twenty-four-hour Sabbath is a big ask for anyone who's just starting to realize that Jesus makes them ENOUGH, so one youth ministry decided to build up gradually to a full-day commitment. The first week they invited students to spend two hours practicing Sabbath, and each week they added another two hours until they reached twenty-four, allowing teenagers to slowly reshape their lives around ample rest.

Creative Connections with Rest

If the young people you're closest to are open to a greater commitment, you can expand their understanding of Sabbath by inviting them to participate alone or with others (including you!) in the following:

- baking
- coloring
- drawing
- hiking and experiencing nature
- practicing yoga
- listening to music
- writing their own psalm
- taking a prayer walk
- sharing a meal with a trusted friend or mentor
- serving someone in need
- praying
- napping
- doing nothing

Not Just "Who Am I?" but "Who Are We?"

As we recenter our identity in Christ, we can't truly answer the question "Who am I?" without also addressing the question "Who are we?"

Many students we interviewed recognized how their view of themselves was influenced by others. Arthur can tell the difference in his identity when he feels safe with those nearby. "I have two personalities. One is really loud—that's who I am during the week. One is really quiet. That is my actual personality. That's who I am at church. The only place I can really recover and trust myself is at church."

Young people's 3 big questions are inextricably connected, refracting both light and shadows onto each other like a prism. In the next two chapters, we explore one of the most influential forces in a young person's identity: their sense of belonging.

Christ-Centered Identity Recap

In this chapter on Christ-centered identity, as well as in chapter 7 on Christ-centered belonging and in chapter 9 on Christ-centered purpose, we provide a handful of summary phrases for you and your teenagers. We've geared these statements to serve not just as a recap but also as reminders of your conversations and connections. Once you have chosen an identity message you want to remember, the next step is to create a system that reminds you of that truth every day.

You and your young people might want to *set a daily alarm on your phones*—to go off perhaps in the morning as you're getting ready or the evening as you're winding down—to remind you to think about one or more of these divine truths.

Or maybe go "low tech" and *write God's better message on an index card* you display on your bathroom mirror, car dashboard, or office bookshelf.

Perhaps you and your students can *take turns texting important messages* to each other, strengthening your mutual commitment to rest in God's ENOUGH-ness.

Whatever you choose, make sure *you* also do whatever you ask of your young people so that you too can share your progress in realizing your true identity.

Here is a list of messages you can draw from:

- I'm ENOUGH because of Jesus.
- Jesus makes what I have, and who I am, *more than* ENOUGH.
- Jesus turns our not-enough into ENOUGH.
- Jesus' generosity can flow through a young person and spread to all generations.
- We cannot tell kids enough that God says they are ENOUGH.
- Sabbath = pray and play.
- On the Sabbath, what will we say yes to? What will we say no to?

REFLECT and APPLY

1. Which of the conversation or Sabbath connection ideas in this chapter would be best for you and the young people you know?

2. What difference might that conversation or connection make in you and in your young people's sense of identity?

3. What might you and your young people have to adjust in your relationships or routines to make time for that change? What would make it worthwhile to make that change?

4. What prayer would you like to offer as you help young people, as well as yourself, understand that God makes us ENOUGH?

PART III

WHERE
DO I FIT?

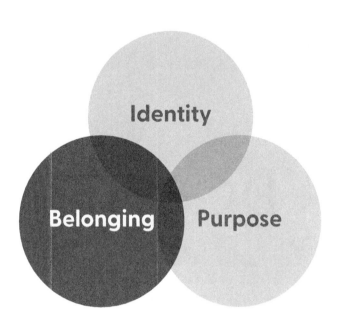

The Big Question of Belonging

Thing is, I've never been older than sixteen. I can't know what it's like to have lived a whole life only to look back and realize I was truly lonely. But I know the flip side of that coin—what it's like to see my life spread out in front of me as a hundred roads to be traveled, and what if I choose the wrong one? Or worse, what if the wrong one is chosen for me, and I get to the end of this road and no one else is there? That fear I know well. And sometimes I think the potential of loneliness is scarier than actual loneliness.

Noah, *The Strange Fascinations of Noah Hypnotik*[1]

Michael has lived in the same farmhouse down a dirt road his entire life. This tall White senior from Michigan drives a lifted pickup truck and goes to a local Christian school—the same one his dad attended. He loves baseball, works on cars, and spends a lot of time outside.

Michael describes being part of his church since "before he was born." In fact, so have both of his parents. And grandparents. As Michael observed, "It's just a family thing, I guess." That "family thing" extends to cousins and people who are like family, given their long-term relationships in this historically Dutch farming community.

Faith devotion is common within that close network. "Most of my family and cousins were brought up with me—Christian school their whole life, church twice on Sunday, the Bible and a devotion at the dinner table. Growing up, I was in everything related to church."

He has a close-knit group of friends at school. "I would never want it to change." The teachers there are not just authority figures but also offer support and tell students, "You can talk to me." And his church "is a tight community, like everybody knows everybody, so when you walk in you just feel like . . . people come to talk to you, so you feel like you are wanted there."

That feeling of being wanted has always characterized Michael's relationships at home too. His mom has been "super supportive, no matter what. I played three sports, and my mom would bring me to all the practices and get me all the equipment. Even if I was not great at what I did, my parents would still support me and want me to succeed in what I liked doing—always ready to help. And my mom is always there to talk and stuff like that, which is huge."

Michael's relationship with his father is also close, and they like to ride ATVs or snowmobiles and hunt together. Sharing a photograph of two snowmobiles on a forest trail, he talked about how meaningful it is to "have a very close relationship with my dad. In this picture, this is his sled in front of mine. I'm doing this with him. I can do this by myself, and he could do it by himself, but we would rather do it together and have fun with each other. It's cool because, as I grow up, he still wants to be part of my life—a big part of my life. That's how I feel accepted."

Like most of his peers, Michael spends a few hours a day on Instagram, Snapchat, TikTok, and text messaging. But unlike most students we interviewed, Michael worries about the downside of technology. "I feel like our security is in technology. You don't want to talk to people, so you just text them or something like that. I just feel like we have lost a sense of having a real relationship with people around us and having face-to-face conversations."

While Michael generally works hard at school and his job, he doesn't feel like he has to work hard in order to belong. He just *belongs*. "Your belonging is your safe place . . . you just feel secure when you belong somewhere."

Defining Belonging: Where Do I Fit?

Belonging is *our connection with others*. It's how we feel like we fit in with groups of people. We might say we "belong" when we're with those who really know, understand, and accept us for who we are.

Belonging is one of the great spiritual hungers of our day. We are a society marked by loneliness and disconnection. We have so many reasons for telling people they don't belong—because of their personality, neighborhood, income, race, ethnicity, immigration status, or disability. We have friends and followers and fans on social media, but these connections often only remind us who *isn't* following us or where we *don't* belong.

We want to belong so badly that we will go to great lengths—even hiding or changing parts of our identity or pursuing a false sense of purpose—to feel it. For teenagers in particular, "Where do I fit?" usually leads among the 3 big questions. They're desperate to belong.

What about Loneliness?

Is this the loneliest generation? Have we reached "epidemic levels"[2] of loneliness in our society?

Maybe.

Loneliness is no small thing. It has the same impact on mortality as smoking fifteen cigarettes a day. It's a better predictor of early death than obesity. So yes, loneliness can kill us.[3] At the same time, all loneliness isn't equal.

Research suggests that while some teenagers feel particularly alone during adolescence, overall some people simply feel lonelier than others. Loneliness is based on how we perceive our relationships—the ones we have versus the ones we wish we had. These discrepancies can be greatest during the teen years; part of growing up is sorting out where we need to forge stronger bonds or when we need to have more realistic expectations for our friendships.[4]

One teenager we know sized this up well on her first day of class at a new school. As she got out of the car, she turned to her dad and said, "Okay, I have three hours to find someone to sit with at lunch."

Sitting by yourself at lunch feels painfully lonely for most teenagers. But some young people can be surrounded by others and still feel lonely. A recent global study revealed that of all generations, loneliness was highest among sixteen- to twenty-four-year-olds, with 40 percent saying they felt lonely often or very often.[5] And a 2019 US-based survey found that Gen Z identifies with loneliness more than any other generation, with more than half feeling as if people

What Is It That Young People Remember the Most about Their High School Ministry?

In our Growing Young research, responses to this question varied from playing silly games at youth retreats to attending big conferences to learning more about their faith. But the number one response young people gave to this question was the ministry's *consistency.* Young people need something stable to come back to when everything else in their lives is in flux.[a]

around them are not really *with* them and that no one really knows them well.[6]

So loneliness is a mixed bag—for young people and for all of us—when it comes to our experiences of belonging. Keeping this in mind, we now turn to the three most common answers we heard to the question "Where do I fit?"

Three Current Answers for Belonging: I Fit . . .

I Fit Where I Feel Safe to Be Me

I fit where I feel comfortable—with people who accept me and don't judge me, where I can be my real self and not fake, where I'm included.

In some ways, safety is part of the very meaning of belonging. It's a basic condition, a prerequisite. Feelings of safety, security, and acceptance are critical to belonging in groups.[7] Students we interviewed used the term *safe* and related synonyms (*secure, shelter, protect*) over one hundred times to describe various aspects of belonging. They also talked about belonging as where they feel comfortable, with people who feel like family.

a. Analysis based on FYI's Growing Young research dataset. Thanks to Daniel Mendoza for this insight.

It's like not having to be fake around certain people, because if you're being fake that's not where you belong, you know? —Hailey

The Power of Friendship

We might be tempted to underestimate the power of friendship for adolescents. That would be a mistake. Friendship is key to answering not only the big question of belonging but also those of identity and purpose. What's more, the holistic health benefits of friendship have been repeatedly supported by research: friends help us live both longer and better. Journalistic researcher Lydia Denworth explored the role of friendship and concluded:

> Having and being a good friend counts for as much or more than the many other achievements we push our kids toward in the classroom, on the basketball court or in the orchestra. Friendship is where kids build social skills—companionship, trust, loyalty, reciprocity and reconciliation—that they can only learn from peer relationships. These are muscles they need to strengthen for adulthood. As they age, strong friendships will be as important for our children's health as diet and exercise.[a]

A number of students in our interviews talked about finding good friends later in high school. Like Armando, whose junior year was a turning point because he finally found a friend group that felt "like family to me. Finding friends like those—it's once in a lifetime." And Hannah, who shared, "In senior year I found my real friends. They were not necessarily the popular people, but genuinely kindhearted. I don't feel like I have to constantly try to impress them, and I'm not afraid they will make fun of me. These are friends who will accept me for whoever I am."

a. Lydia Denworth, "How Monkeys Taught Me to Appreciate Teen Sleepovers," *New York Times*, February 4, 2020, https://www.nytimes.com/2020/02/04/well/family/teenagers-friendships-sleepovers-video-games-parenting.html. Denworth is the author of *Friendship: The Evolution, Biology, and Extraordinary Power of Life's Fundamental Bond* (New York: Norton, 2020).

Arthur talked about safety as a word that "kind of encompasses everything, because it is the one place I can return to and still be loved regardless of whatever I do, whatever I say."

Janelle reflected, "If I'm in an unknown situation or place, it naturally feels uneasy. So it's not safe. Like I'm safe from danger, but not safe to be who I am or to express myself in the way that I want." She contrasted this with being at home: "I can be myself there."

This underscores the link between identity and belonging, a theme we will see elsewhere in this chapter. When I really belong, it's not just about fitting in. It's about bringing my real self to the table and not just the version others want to see.

Hailey frequently feels as though she has to present a particular version of herself in order to fit in with her friends. She shared, "Even though I enjoy hanging out with friends, sometimes I feel like I need to say something to be funny. But then if no one laughs, I'm like, *Oh no, I'm not a good friend.* Sometimes it's overwhelming to try to be a friend, and I think, *I can't say this* or *If I do that, they're not going to like me.*"

For Janelle and many of our interview participants, home life was a significant source of belonging. But for others, family didn't feel so safe.

We mentioned in chapter 5 that Sebastian had experienced abuse at home. He painfully recalled, "Being abused by my

NOTE: If a young person discloses abuse of any type in a conversation with you, in particular if the teenager is in current danger, please reach out for additional support. Depending on your state and local guidelines, you may be a mandated reporter, meaning you are obligated to share suspected or alleged abuse with authorities. Please consult your supervisor (whether you serve in a paid or volunteer role) if you are unsure about abuse protocols in your context. You can also call or text the Childhelp National Child Abuse Hotline at 1-800-4-A-CHILD (1-800-422-4453) for guidance or visit childwelfare.gov.

dad made me want to question my belonging everywhere I went. I had to make sure this was a place I belonged and that these were people who actually accepted me for who I am, because he didn't accept me at all. Even now, if I'm going to be in a new environment, I have to first make sure they accept me."

Indeed, not belonging in our families is one of the most painful hurts we can experience.

I Fit Where We Share _____.

> I fit where we have shared experiences, where we have the same values and priorities, where we have worked together on something, where we like the same music or use similar language.

Michael, whom we met at the start of this chapter, talked about belonging with his friends because they share so much in common. "It's great just being able to sit around and talk about things that don't matter or things that do matter. Anything in general, just sitting around and talking. Having different views on things, but also believing the same stuff in general. And being sarcastic with each other—just messing around. I think that is kind of a cool thing."

We frequently heard belonging described as simply *being together*. We also heard a lot about shared experiences that create belonging: running on the same cross-country team, being in a school club, going on a church retreat, or even listening to the same music.

Of course, these very experiences that foster belonging for some can make those who don't share them feel even more left out. One senior reflected, "A lot of times when I was in middle school, I tried to learn song lyrics to make

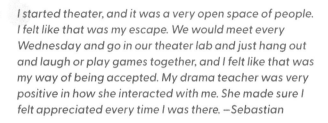

I started theater, and it was a very open space of people. I felt like that was my escape. We would meet every Wednesday and go in our theater lab and just hang out and laugh or play games together, and I felt like that was my way of being accepted. My drama teacher was very positive in how she interacted with me. She made sure I felt appreciated every time I was there. —Sebastian

friends. But as soon as a new song came out and I didn't know it, we weren't friends anymore. I didn't know how that worked."

It can be helpful to think about these aspects of shared experience like a topography of belonging—a landscape teenagers traverse in search of their fit. Young people constantly navigate multiple groups and relationships simultaneously, whether due to divorce, race, migration, or just the difference between church, family, and school. These can feel like disparate locations on a young person's belonging map.

It's not uncommon for a young person to feel as though they're constantly shifting *who they are* for different audiences because they desperately *want to belong* in each group. But as they move from place to place on the map, they belong in different ways. As we were processing interview insights, Montague Williams, an advisor for this project, suggested, "This whole work of belonging is about trying out different versions of 'we.'" Sometimes the "me" changes for each "we." The student who was confused about the connection between song lyrics and friends illustrates that true belonging—being known, understood, and accepted—can feel just plain elusive, like a hidden spot off the grid.

Being on the outside is hard. Steve is a senior from North Carolina who talked insightfully about exclusion with Andy Jung, his interviewer.

> ANDY: Now think about a time you felt left out or excluded. Tell me a little bit about that experience.
>
> STEVE: I'd have to say football. The team is close, but I am not really close with the team. All of them hang out on the weekends. They do stuff together. I just don't hang out with them, because none of my friends—my close, close friends—play this sport. So whenever they are going to a party or to get food, I don't get invited or asked if I'm going. I don't feel like that is really who I am or who I need to be with, but I still feel excluded.
>
> ANDY: Do you feel that was a decision *you* made, or was that a decision made by the rest of the team?
>
> STEVE: I think it was made for me, because I would love to hang out with the guys, you know—go do whatever they're going to do. I just haven't been …
>
> ANDY: Just have never been included?
>
> STEVE: Right. Never been included.

Many teenagers who struggle to find shared experiences with peers in their local community look online for support (as do some of their parents). This is especially true for LGBTQ young people who feel rejected at school, home, or church—or all three. Inclusive virtual environments have been shown to increase these teenagers' sense of belonging.[8]

Taylor, who identifies as gender nonbinary, hasn't had to find acceptance only through meeting other teenagers online but does worry about belonging when not around close friends—most of whom are also "part of the LGBTQ community." Taylor shared, "I worry when I meet new people that they're not going to respect my identity or that they will be rude to me. I have the constant fear of being misgendered on purpose. I think that's why I hang out with my friends so much; that is where I know I belong."

I Would Fit If I Were White ... or If I Had Been Born Here

We would be missing a key element in the experience of half of this generation if we didn't name how culture and race impact belonging. Implicitly or explicitly, US young people of color and Indigenous youth often hear the message that they fit only if they are White. Immigrant and refugee youth may also face barriers to belonging, depending on their familiarity with dominant US culture, English language fluency, and family citizenship status.

This is a well-researched phenomenon known as "belonging uncertainty."[a] Belonging uncertainty happens when someone in a particular group questions whether they belong in a social setting such as school, a team, work, or church. In chapter 2, we shared Janelle's experience of being good at school but hearing from peers that Black kids aren't supposed to be smart, and in chapter 4, we noted Daniel's experience of not fitting in with Black teammates because he doesn't speak in a certain manner and is biracial. Arthur also experienced this belonging uncertainty as a result of moving internationally multiple times as a child: from Korea to China, back to Korea, then to the US, each move requiring cultural adaptation.

Discrimination affects teenagers in many ways, one of which is a feeling of "I don't really fit here." For Janelle, that could translate as "AP classes are for White kids," and for Daniel as "not being Black enough" on the basketball court. That sort of uncertainty can negatively impact both academics and health. The good news is that when students are reassured they do belong, they are more protected against negative stereotypes, are more likely to earn higher grades, and remain healthier overall.[b]

a. Gregory M. Walton and Geoffrey L. Cohen, "A Question of Belonging: Race, Social Fit, and Achievement," *Journal of Personality and Social Psychology* 92, no. 1 (2007): 82–96; and Gregory M. Walton and Geoffrey L. Cohen, "A Brief Social-Belonging Intervention Improves Academic and Health Outcomes of Minority Students," *Science* 331, no. 6023 (2011): 1447–51.
b. Walton and Cohen, "A Brief Social-Belonging Intervention," 1447.

I Fit Where I Feel Like I'm Needed

I fit where I have to help out in some way, when I'm needed.

Daniel describes an interplay between belonging and responsibility. His family attends a predominantly Asian American church where Daniel is very involved. Far from being a passive participant, he knows his church needs him to help out. But Daniel doesn't talk about it like an obligation—it's just part of what it means to belong.

At home, Daniel often has to help take care of his younger sister and his dad, who struggles with multiple health issues, while his mom juggles several jobs. His mom talks about "sticking together" as a family value and being a "team." Daniel knows he's needed, and he has had to bear the weight of adult responsibility early—especially when they weathered a series of evictions and moves. But he describes family hardship as part of what has cemented their belonging. There is no question they need one another.

One of the ways researchers talk about belonging is seeing ourselves as integral parts of the systems that surround us—relationships, organizations, and cultural environments.[9] So it's natural for young people to feel like they belong when they know they're needed in some way. Being needed can feel good.

But there's a darker side to fitting where we're needed. Sometimes it can feel like belonging is conditional. It can add pressure and expectations. It can leave teenagers feeling as if they're never free to just "be" in a world that always needs them to "do."

Teenagers' Complicated Relationship with Tech

America now divides into two classes: those who have lived with social media–laden smartphones since childhood, and the rest of us. Note how we elders are now the exception, rather than the rule, since our time will never come again. A profound and irreversible change in the grain of ordinary life has taken place, and the kids who have swiped iPads from infancy are now old enough to be forming significant political communities online. Their socially augmented reality has arrived, but our understanding of their ways has not kept pace.

Josephine Livingstone[a]

For "the rest of us," teenagers' tech use can raise all kinds of concerns. We worry about the effects of gaming too much, posting on social media too much, texting too much, and staring at screens too much. Some of these fears are certainly valid.

Others are a function of generational differences. Even if we feel relatively tech-savvy and comfortable with a variety of devices and platforms, those of us over thirty-five are still not indigenously digital. We immigrated from another world altogether. We can work to empathize with young people, but we haven't shared their experiences.

One of adults' concerns about tech use is its impact on relationships. So how does belonging look different in the digital world?

First, as we mention in this chapter, young people who feel ostracized in their communities can find belonging in virtual contexts with others who share their particular interests, medical or psychological diagnosis, sexual orientation, or gender identity. For example, advocacy organizations such as the National Eating Disorder Association provide online communities for struggling youth.[b]

Second, when social media is used for enhancing existing relationships, it can become a useful tool for reducing loneliness. For most teenagers, there is a big overlap between real and virtual relationships. Staying in touch through social media with friends from school, church, sports, or camp has been shown to increase belongingness.[c] This was especially helpful for young people (and perhaps all generations) during the COVID-19 pandemic as digital means of communication became a lifeline for belonging.[d]

But the opposite also happens. When social media is used as an escape from the social pain of interactions, it can have a negative impact. Young people may hide in plain sight on devices and protect themselves from rejection, but it comes at the cost of increasing loneliness.[e]

Third, many Gen Z youth see conversation as a seamless event across platforms. They might be connecting with the same friends in multiple places simultaneously, including IRL (In Real Life), without a second thought that this is unusual.[f] Lilly shared, "It's so weird, because I have my Kakao group chats with my friends, but then I also talk to them on Snapchat and Instagram. So I'll send my friend a post of a meme on Instagram and then send the same friend a TikTok through Snapchat. Then she will respond to both. We're having two separate conversations at the same time on two different social media platforms."

The complicated advantages and disadvantages of technology are well described by Arthur: "Social media and texting help me talk with my friends and get closer to them. But social media also helps people badmouth others, which people have done to me. [Laughs.] So I cut off my social contact with those people. So yeah, for me, it goes both ways. I agree that it can do good, but it can potentially also do bad."

a. Josephine Livingstone, "*Jawline* Explores the Teenage Dream of Social Media," *New Republic*, August 22, 2019, https://newrepublic.com/article/154824/jawline-explores-teenage-dream-social-media.

b. See the resources available at nationaleatingdisorders.org.

c. Katie Davis, "Friendship 2.0: Adolescents' Experiences of Belonging and Self-Disclosure Online," *Journal of Adolescence* 35, no. 6 (2012): 1527–36; and Rebecca Nowland, Elizabeth A. Necka, and John T. Cacioppo, "Loneliness and Social Internet Use: Pathways to Reconnection in a Digital World?" *Perspectives on Psychological Science* 13, no. 1 (January 2018): 70–87.

d. Candice L. Odgers and Michael B. Robb, *Tweens, Teens, Tech, and Mental Health* (San Francisco: Common Sense Media, 2020).

e. Nowland, Necka, and Cacioppo, "Loneliness and Social Internet Use," 70. Though note that studies have been unable to clearly link tech use itself with loneliness. Both very heavy social media users and those who don't use it at all report similar rates of loneliness. Alexa Hagerty, "Community Can Offer a Cure to Our Technology Addictions," *Pacific Standard*, May 6, 2019, https://psmag.com/ideas/how-community-can-offer-a-cure-to-our-technology-addictions.

f. Thanks to Joi Freeman of Remnant Strategy for this insight. Find more of Joi's work on Gen Z at remnant strategy.com.

Big Question	Focus	Description	Current Answers	Christ-Centered Answer
Who am I?	Identity	Our view of ourselves	*I am* ... • what others expect. • not _____ enough. • my image. • more than my label.	I'm ENOUGH be-cause of Jesus.
Where do I fit?	Belonging	Our con-nection with others	*I fit* ... • where I feel safe to be me. • where we share _____. • where I feel like I'm needed.	

Remembering Where We Fit When We Were Teenagers

Garrison Hayes serves as pastor for generational ministries at Community Praise Church in Alexandria, Virginia. He interviewed teenagers on the East Coast for this project, and I (Brad) caught up with him to explore themes of belonging—both in his life and with students in his ministry.

BRAD: When you were a teenager, how do you remember wrestling with the question of belonging: Where do I fit?

GARRISON: I was born in 1990, so my teenage years happened as the internet was really becoming a thing. I started a YouTube channel and built what I thought was a really cool following of a thousand people, and I was like, "I'm famous now!" I was wrestling with identity and belonging in both real life and on the internet, curating this person I thought I wanted to be.

I didn't feel like I really belonged at my family's conservative Christian church, in part because of the way people viewed filmmaking. I wrestled with having a sense of calling, but not the approval of my community. So I found belonging on the internet among a community of people who were also making films. I didn't feel like I had to explain anything in order to be accepted there.

BRAD: What were some other influences on your sense of belonging during those years?

GARRISON: At the risk of sounding contradictory, my pastor was a huge influence. I felt really connected to him and his charisma and way of communicating. I think I tried to take that to the internet when I was making videos.

  Some of my older cousins mentored me and loved me through my teen years—they always let me be myself. So did my grandmother, my nana. She moved in with us when I was six, so I don't have a lot of memories without her being part of the family. I've always felt a profound sense of belonging with her. To this day, anywhere she is, that's where I want to be.

BRAD: What do you wish adults had done when you were a young person that would have increased your sense of belonging?

GARRISON: I wish they had asked me what I wanted to do in life and who I wanted to be. I wish they had been more curious about who I was and less exacting on who I should be according to their theology, tradition, practice, and ideas about the world. I think if I'd had more curious adults in my life, I would have felt much more like I fit; I would've felt at least heard.

BRAD: Often teenagers feel as if they don't really belong even in their own families. Thinking about parents and caregivers, what do you wish they would do to increase a sense of belonging, that sense of fitting in our families?

GARRISON: I try to have consideration for privilege and what people are able to give and do, but I really wish more parents invited their teenagers to have some sort of say in what happens in the home. Parents have big decisions to make that children can't always give input on. But they can invite them to have input in the meal that night or what they're watching or what they're doing this week. Even on that level, it's something that gives kids a sense of ownership in the home. I think ownership builds belonging.

BRAD: What have you learned about teenagers and belonging as an interviewer for this project that you're taking back to your ministry?

GARRISON: I think most teenagers feel as though they belong with their friends, particularly people who laugh at the same things, believe the same things, and who are willing to allow them to be authentically themselves. If they feel that they are being themselves today, they feel as though they belong. It's been valuable for me as a youth leader to remember I was like that as well—and belonging is a desire we never really lose.

You know, I can't help but consider the moment we're living in and all we're facing, especially in light of racial injustice. The search to belong is intersecting with current events and what's happening in a young person's life. I think the need for authenticity is heightened. I had a conversation with some of my teens about where they are and how they're feeling about everything going on around us. What kept coming to the surface is that they wanted to share anger and frustration and confusion without someone trying to dictate how those emotions should be felt or expressed.

As we're having critical conversations on race and justice and equity, I think it's important for our students to feel heard, listened to, and accepted for who they are and what they believe. Being able to level with them without trying to control their thoughts is really important in fostering a sense of belonging.

I Belong . . . for Now

Earlier in this chapter we heard from Hannah, who described making close friends her senior year of high school. For students like Hannah, sometimes earlier experiences of rejection shape the way they later find true belonging. Hannah talked about being bullied in middle school as a precursor to how she sees people now.

> In junior high, I would spend all of my lunches and breaks in the bathroom stalls, or I would pretend to be sick and my grandpa would pick me up—to the point that the nurses were like my friends. I think going through that taught me a lot of compassion. Instead of being quick to judge others, I want to get to know them and give them the benefit of the doubt. I do my best to reach out to people.

As with identity, teenagers are figuring belonging out as they go. It has a temporary nature to it because young people's lives are in motion. They must constantly negotiate where they fit.

Much of the time, young people qualify "I belong" with "for now."

We all long for a more permanent sense of belonging—one that isn't qualified by whether we feel safe enough to be ourselves, we share the right things, or we're needed. In the next chapter, we will explore a Christ-centered response to the question "Where do I fit?" and share ideas to help the young people in your life say an everyday "Yes" to Jesus' better answer.

REFLECT and APPLY

1. Below are the three current answers young people commonly use to define their belonging. To help you empathize with today's teenagers, reflect on yourself as a teenager. Rank the answers from 1 to 3, giving a 1 to the answer that was most common for you and a 3 to the one you identified with least.

   - _____ I fit where I feel safe to be me.

   - _____ I fit where we share _____ .

   - _____ I fit where I feel like I'm needed.

2. Looking back, what was helpful about the answers you gravitated toward?

3. What was perhaps hurtful to you or others?

4. Now think about a young person you know and repeat the same process, placing a 1 next to their most common belonging answer and a 3 next to their least common belonging answer.

- _____ I fit where I feel safe to be me.

- _____ I fit where we share _____.

- _____ I fit where I feel like I'm needed.

5. Acceptance and inclusion are critical to feeling safe enough to belong with others. On a scale of 1 to 10, with 1 being "not much at all" and 10 being "a lot," how much do you think the young person you have in mind feels accepted and included by peers in their life? Are there certain contexts where that number would be much higher or much lower? How would they rate the acceptance they feel from adults in their life—parents, teachers, coaches, faith leaders, mentors?

6. In the next chapter, we will explore a better Christ-centered answer to teenagers' deep desire for belonging. What ideas do you already have for a better answer to the big question "Where do I fit?"

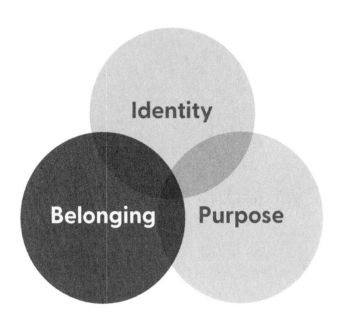

WITH:
Jesus' Better Answer

Stop walking through the world looking for confirmation that you don't belong. You will always find it because you've made that your mission. Stop scouring people's faces for evidence that you're not enough. You will always find it because that's your goal. . . . No one belongs here more than you.

Brené Brown[1]

What does it feel like to live as if "no one belongs here more than you"? To know you are welcomed, accepted, and embraced as "one of us," no matter what?

Despite rejection in other circles, sixteen-year-old Sue found the answer in her church youth group and on her swim team. As an Asian American in a predominantly White suburban community and church in the South, she doesn't always feel like she belongs. When we asked, "Where do you feel like yourself the most?" she responded enthusiastically:

Oh, with the youth group definitely. When I'm with my youth group, I can be that person who doesn't care about what other people think. There was this one day when I walked into youth group and all of my friends were there, and they all turned around and yelled, "SUE!" And that just made me feel like these are the people who care about me and support me. Because I've been left out before and I know how that feels, and so the difference—I can see it and feel it. I can still be myself, because I know that no matter what I say, they'll still like me.

Sue contrasted these experiences with feelings of not belonging: "I guess there are times when I just get down and feel like nobody likes me. Like when I'm in a group of friends and I feel sort of left out or something. Then I get really sad, like, 'Nobody wants to hang out with me.'"

When asked to describe God, Sue immediately connected God with a sense of belonging. She shared, "The first word that comes to mind is 'safe.' I feel safe and I feel comforted. And then I would describe God as a father figure. He is there to support you and to be there for you whenever you need it. And somebody who is always by your side—a best friend and father."

Sue's youth group has embodied the kind of holy safety that frees her to be herself without having to earn a seat at the table, and this embrace from her faith community has helped her say an everyday "Yes" to Jesus. Like most of the teenagers we interviewed, Sue is being formed through belonging with God's people.

The Christ-Centered Answer in One Word: WITH

Young people like Sue are hungry to be accepted, known, and welcomed for who they are. As they search for an answer to the big question "Where do I fit?" we can help them discover the Christ-centered answer: *I belong* with *God's people.*

WITH.

God has created us to be in community WITH God and WITH others through Jesus. We don't have to earn love, acceptance, or our place in the body of Christ. We belong to God and to one another. We are not alone.

We are family.

WITH is our core word for belonging because it symbolizes the heart of God to be near us, among us, and close to us as beloved children for whom God's heart beats. God is WITH us and our young people—no matter what.

This is better news than just feeling "safe to be me." Safety is fleeting, conditional, and subject to how others make us feel. Make no mistake: safety is *critical* for relational connection. But our truest belonging is not dependent on the success or failure of others to live it out. It has already been decided by the unconditional love of God.

As many of our teenagers have painfully discovered, those who initially make us feel like we belong can (and have) regularly let us down, making belonging perhaps the most complicated of the 3 big questions.

God Is WITH Us—We Are WITH One Another: John 13–17

Jesus' entire life on earth put flesh on God's commitment to be WITH us and is a model for how we are to be WITH

If you're tracking FYI's work closely, you know that WITH is a theme we really like! I (Kara) wrote a book with Steve Argue entitled *Growing With*, which explores how parents can be "with" teenagers and emerging adults more intentionally. To find out more, visit growingwithbook.com.

one another. But perhaps no other portion of the Gospels captures WITH better than John chapters13–17. The introduction for this entire section is framed in love, which is the heart of belonging: "Having loved his own who were in the world, he loved them to the end" (John 13:1).

It's Passover. The small band of disciples gathers with Jesus for the meal. This would all be as usual—but Jesus disrupts the pattern. Taking these chapters as a whole, we see that Jesus gives us a better answer to the big question of belonging.

We Are Friends Who Wash Feet and Share Tables

The Master takes on the physical job of a servant, washing dirty feet. Jesus had spent a few years with his closest followers doing all kinds of things together, but this was new. It was absurd. In this profoundly physical, humble, even humiliating act, Jesus kneels with the posture of a servant and pours water over each road-weary foot.

Then he tells the disciples to keep doing this for each other (John 13:14–15). That extends out to us—an invitation to take the same posture of being WITH one another by serving one another.

Without missing a beat, Jesus sits at a table with his friends—even friends who would betray and desert him—and hands out bread. This meal, which we often repeat as the Lord's Supper, or Eucharist, is a meal not only for those whose faith is strong but also for the struggling, a meal for the broken and uncertain. A meal for those who would be Jesus' imperfect friends.

While both washing feet and eating with his disciples, Jesus talks about friendship and love and how he's going to be WITH them even when he is absent. Fuller New Testament professor Tommy Givens links all of this to the power of friendship to connect us.

> If the gospel is especially about the way God empowers people to love one another, then friendship names this power at its most intimate. Friendship is what Jesus told his disciples he was teaching them when he washed their feet and then loved them to the death. Friendship is not simply something modeled for us in a few stories of the Bible or one of many topics covered in the Bible. It is the way God has drawn near to us, through much suffering, so that we are able to draw near to God and to one another.[2]

Christian community is fundamentally marked by a relational God who is willing to be WITH us—stinky feet and all.[3]

We Are Known by Our Love

The best testimony to the truth of the gospel is the quality of our life together.

Christine Pohl[4]

John puts this foot washing and eating in the context of the *fullness of God's love* through Jesus. Then Jesus roots all of our belonging in unconditional love, declaring, "A new command I give you: Love one another. As I have loved you, so you must love one another. By this everyone will know that you are my disciples, if you love one another" (John 13:34–35).

Jesus uses strong language here—the language of command. He draws on his authority to say something unpopular and hard to live out.

Unconditional love is not only the signature mark of our relationships in the community of Jesus; it's also magnetic to

outsiders. Unlike what teenagers normally settle for, unconditional love is not earned and is not based on performance,
sharing the same experiences, or fitting in. Willie James Jennings writes, "What will you do if I join you at the body of
Jesus and fall in love with your God and with you? . . . This
is the most terrifying aspect of interruption: love."[5]

We Belong WITH the Triune God

Continuing in John's account of Jesus' last night, in chapter 14 Jesus promises rooms in God's house that his disciples
will share with him. Jesus isn't very descriptive about what
this will be like or when it will happen, but he makes it
clear that no one will be alone while they wait. The Spirit
is promised as the comforter and advocate who "lives with
you and will be in you" (v. 17).

Catholic writer Carl McColman draws on the early Christian image of the members of the Trinity in a dance to illustrate how the Spirit inhabits us.

> God is in us, because we are in Christ. As members of the
> mystical body, Christians actually partake in the divine na-
> ture of the Trinity. We do not merely *watch* the dance, we
> *dance* the dance. We join hands with Christ and the Spirit
> flows through us and between us and our feet move always
> in the loving embrace of the Father. In that we are members
> of the mystical body of Christ, we see the joyful love of the
> Father through the eyes of the Son. And with every breath,
> we breathe the Holy Spirit.[6]

The Holy Spirit is God WITH us every moment. Jesus
assures us of this union: "I am in my Father, and you are
in me, and I am in you" (v. 20). He repeats this imagery of

> *We all come from very different backgrounds, but we all still love each other. And we might argue sometimes, but at the end of the day, we are like a family. —Natalie*

interconnectedness over and over, driving home the point: stay connected, remain, abide in me (John 15:4–10). This WITH-ness is an avenue for joy (v. 11), friendship with God (v. 15), and peace in the face of adversity (16:33).

Even when the earthly community of the church fails us, we can hold to the promise of God's Spirit WITH us and in us. But Jesus hopes the church will be something more.

We Belong WITH One Another as the Church

In John 17, as Jesus begins to pray, he looks ahead to the future—that all of us may be one and that this oneness would be evidence to the world that Jesus loves us and that God sent Jesus to be with us. Through the church, we choose to move toward one another in Jesus' name.[7]

This unity creates a sign to the world through the ways we live and treat one another as brothers and sisters,[8] strengthening one another rather than tearing one another apart. As my (Brad's) friend Warren is fond of saying to our church, this means we are much more than "just a loose association of the independently spiritual." We are one body. We depend on one another and experience God through one another.

That's what it means to be God's people.

This radical version of belonging reinforces our worth. During the course of this research, I (Brad) talked at length with a therapist who works with teenagers. She told me that in her practice, she sees the following pattern over and over: if young people feel belonging, they feel worthy of love. Our inclusivity confers value to the teenagers among us.

It's important to note here that *unity* is not the same as *uniformity*.[9] Our unity in Christ does not erase diversity. Rather, it affirms and even demands diversity for the flourishing of the world. Our distinctive voices allow God's truth to be told in more than one way.[10] Jesus stands against and overcomes exclusivism—whether by race, ethnicity, gender, or age.[11] We need all of us in order to be fully formed in the image of Christ.

Big Question	Focus	Description	Current Answers	Christ-Centered Answer
Who am I?	Identity	Our view of ourselves	I am… ▪ what others expect. ▪ not ____ enough. ▪ my image. ▪ more than my label.	I'm ENOUGH because of Jesus.
Where do I fit?	Belonging	Our connection with others	I fit… ▪ where I feel safe to be me. ▪ where we share ____. ▪ where I feel like I'm needed.	I belong WITH God's people.

WITH Gets Practical—Conversations and Connections

We settle for the illusion of separation when we are endlessly asked to enter into kinship with all.

Gregory Boyle[12]

How can we help young people move from knowing God is WITH them in some mystical way to saying an everyday "Yes" to belonging WITH God's people concretely? Try these conversations and connections with the teenagers in your life.

Conversations about Belonging

A Conversation Exploring Belonging—No Matter What

Help a teenager evaluate belonging in different contexts and identify where they feel like they belong, no matter what.

NOW

1. When do you feel the most comfortable around other people?
2. When do you feel the least comfortable?
3. Who are the people in your life who make you feel like you fit—like you belong?
4. Where do you feel like you belong, no matter what?

GOD

5. How do you know you belong WITH God's people?
6. What does our church or ministry do to help you feel like you belong unconditionally? What do you wish our church or ministry would do differently?

HOW

7. What do you need from others to really know that you belong WITH them, no matter what?
8. What can you do to help others know they belong, no matter what?
9. Can we think of some ideas together for how I can remind you that you belong WITH God's people?

A Conversation for When a Teenager Doesn't Want to Go to Church

"I'm not going to church."

We've all heard these words from a teenager in our family or ministry. The last thing we want is to say or do something that pushes them further away from the faith community. Here are some prompts to help you make headway in what's often a dead-end conversation.

NOW

1. What makes you not want to go to church?

2. What do you wish was different?

3. Who matters to you at church?

GOD

4. Here's what church has meant to me . . . (share a brief testimony focused on belonging).

5. How has God used someone else at church in your life?

6. I wonder how God could work through your frustrations with church to bring something new?

7. I wonder how church could be more meaningful for you?

HOW

8. Is there a pastor or leader at church with whom you can share how you're feeling? What do you think you would gain? What might you lose?

9. When it comes to church, what would help you feel like you belong?

10. What is one way I can help you reengage with church?

11. What is one thing you can try for the next few weeks that might make your experience of church different?

Conversations about Repair WITH One Another

A friend once confided, "In a family like ours, we say it's all about repair."

This friend and her husband both grew up in dysfunctional families. Despite doing a lot of work on healthier relating and conflict management in adulthood, they still experience mistakes, blowups, and catastrophic moments in their marriage and parenting. They've made "It's all about repair" a mantra in the wake of these waves.

> If we have no peace, it is because we have forgotten that we belong to each other.
>
> Mother Teresa[13]

Repair is a critical skill: knowing how to mend fractured relationships before they become deep breaks; knowing how to confess our mistakes to one another and ask for forgiveness. While some relationship problems need space or outside intervention—particularly when emotional or physical abuse is involved—we can help teenagers process and walk through their typical struggles with a little support.

NOW

1. Tell me more about what happened in this relationship.
2. What hurts most right now?
3. What would you want to hear an apology for?
4. What might you need to apologize for?

GOD

5. What would it look like for God to bring healing to this relationship?

6. Forgiveness is about setting free—both the person you're forgiving and yourself. How would you be different if you were free from holding resentment? How would the other person be free?

7. How would other relationships around both of you look different if this relationship was repaired?

HOW

8. What could repenting or forgiving look like in practice? Can you imagine what you'd say or do?

9. [If the student needs to apologize and repent] How will you apologize? Would you practice with me?

10. [If the student needs to forgive] How will you acknowledge the hurt and still forgive? Will you practice with me?

11. What else needs to happen to repair this relationship?

12. If the other person isn't interested in forgiveness or repair, what can you do to heal without them?

Conversations about WITH Elsewhere in the Bible

Scripture sings of belonging, particularly as the New Testament makes a turn toward answering the question "What—and who—is the church?" Along with John 13–17, the following passages can be compelling to meditate on, memorize, send by text, or compile into a small group or youth ministry teaching series.

- Matthew 1:18–25, especially verse 23: At Jesus' entry into the world as an infant, he is proclaimed Immanuel, God WITH us.

- John 1:1–14, especially verse 14: Jesus, the eternal Word, was WITH God in the beginning and took on flesh to be WITH us.

- Acts 2:42–47: The newly formed first church gathered WITH one another daily to pray, share meals, and share with anyone in need.

- Acts 16:6–15, especially verse 15: The church in Philippi is found and led by Lydia, a new gentile believer who wondered if she belonged WITH God's people too.

- Acts 17:22–28, especially verse 26: Paul says in Athens that God made all people from one ancestor, a reminder that we belong WITH one another. (This was one of the most quoted texts during the US civil rights movement of the 1960s.)[14]

- Romans 12:3–8; 1 Corinthians 12:12–31; Ephesians 4:1–16: The "body of Christ" passages affirm over and over that we all belong WITH one another and indeed belong *to* one another (Rom. 12:5) in the body of Christ.

- Galatians 3:26–29, especially verse 28: Paul declares that in spite of our differences, we are all one WITH each other in Christ Jesus.

- Revelation 7:9–10: This is a glorious vision of a massive intercultural celebration WITH God's people around the throne of the Lamb at the end of time.

Hospitality-Focused Connections about Belonging

> Our lives are knit together not so much by intense feeling as by shared history, tasks, commitments, stories, and sacrifices.
>
> Christine Pohl[15]

Hospitality is a term we often reduce to mean "having someone over for dinner" or maybe to refer to the hotel or restaurant industry. But in our rich Christian tradition of discipleship, hospitality means so much more. It means making room for others. Welcoming the stranger. Saying "you belong here" to someone who doesn't expect it.

Or as our colleague Scott Cormode likes to say, *hospitality means giving the privileges of insiders to outsiders.*[16]

Hospitality is offering community to those who haven't earned it. In fact, all of human life begins with God's act of hospitality—with God making a place for us in the newly created world. Theologian Miroslav Volf says we practice hospitality because we were made to emulate God. He writes, "Having been embraced by God, we must make space for others and invite them in—even our enemies."[17]

Deuteronomy 10:19 instructs God's people: "You shall also love the stranger, for you were strangers in the land of Egypt" (NRSV). And later in the Old Testament, God's prophets remind the people that God will judge them by their care for widows, orphans, and immigrants—that is, by their treatment of outsiders.

In the New Testament, Jesus both practiced hospitality and received it. He ate with "sinners." One of the primary reasons the gospel spread was because Christians practiced a new kind of hospitality—welcoming not just important people but even the most marginalized. This was how the early church developed a reputation of love.

Christian hospitality is reciprocal—the blessing flows in both directions, not just from host to guest. Sharing food is certainly part of hospitality, but in our relationships, homes, and churches, we're invited to lean into a vision of hospitality that is much greater. Here are some ways we can foster hospitality-focused connections with teenagers as part of our everyday "Yes" to God.

Hospitable Connections WITH Church

It's hard to belong to any community—including a faith community—without shared context and shared experience. Few corporate activities hold power to hospitably connect us to one another like the rituals associated with worship: singing, praying, reciting creeds, taking communion, witnessing baptism, kneeling, raising our hands, giving and receiving hugs.

These interactions can be hard for introverts or young people with social anxiety. Showing up can also be risky because of race, culture, gender, lifestyle, or other background. Here are a few ideas to help you practice hospitality to teenagers in worship.

- *Notice them*: We said in chapter 2 that teenagers want to be seen and heard. From a warm welcome at the door to a mention of the teenage experience in a sermon, let young people know they are noticed. It matters to teenagers to be welcomed by other teenagers, so work with committed youth to intentionally reach out to those who are new or on the margins.

- *Involve them*: Nothing cements a young person's connection to church like being given a job to do.[18] Involve teenagers in any role you would involve adults—from up-front leadership and ministry with children to behind-the-scenes work and serving senior adults.

- *Give them significance*: Communicate to teenagers, "We are not all of who we are without you." Repeat the message over and over that they are necessary and indispensable in the body of Christ.

- *Make worship meaningful*: No one likes being bored at church. But the antidote to uninteresting services isn't entertainment—it's *meaning*. Try this: for everything your church does as part of weekly worship, ask "What does it mean?" and "How does it help us make meaning?" Sometimes explaining a practice can open it up to a teenager who has shuffled through it on autopilot in the past. Start by listing typical components of your worship and imagining creative ways to reintroduce them.

- *Connect virtually*: Largely initiated by the COVID-19 pandemic, most churches are supplementing their in-person hospitality with better digitally fueled belonging. Meeting virtually often requires more effort to reinforce we are WITH one another, but it can be

---

At our church, we call each other by "brother" or "sister" because we are all brothers and sisters in Christ—because God made us all equal. We treat each other like family. That's how the church should be, being a whole family in Christ. We're very connected. —Daniel

For Leaders: Connections WITH Teenagers Who Have Special Needs

About one out of six children and teenagers has been diagnosed with a developmental disability of some kind, one out of fifty-four specifically with Autism Spectrum Disorder. These numbers have been rising steadily the past two decades.[a] That means that most of us know a young person who lives with special needs. Leaders often wonder what to do in response to students' needs and how to create inclusive, hospitable environments in which they can thrive as part of the body.

Autism often presents itself in the form of awkward social interactions and unexpected behaviors, which can create unique ministry challenges when so much revolves around personal connection. While the strategies that work for one individual may not work for another, expert Amy Fenton Lee has offered the following tips for creating more inclusive environments for these young people in our midst:

- Develop good relationships with parents, starting with lots of listening, to build trust and partnership.
- Create a web of adult support around students, training your entire volunteer team in inclusive best practices.
- Prepare students ahead of time for what to expect in gatherings in order to reduce the likelihood of unsettling surprises.
- Create printed guidelines for each ministry setting, which can be especially helpful for kids who don't easily follow social cues and unwritten rules of play.
- Facilitate interactions for students who struggle to communicate, modeling conversations for both the student and their peers.
- Find places for students to serve. Just like any young person, a teenager with special needs has gifts, skills, and interests to invest in the church and community.
- Learn from them! Young people with special needs have so much to teach the church when we are open to learning from their perspectives.[b]

a. "Data & Statistics on Autism Spectrum Disorder," June 16, 2020, Centers for Disease Control and Prevention, https://www.cdc.gov/ncbddd/autism/data.html.

b. Adapted from Amy Fenton Lee's two-article series, "Refusing to Ignore Teenagers with Special Needs," Fuller Youth Institute, September 14, 2014, https://fulleryouthinstitute.org/articles/special-needs; and "Sticky Faith and Special Needs," Fuller Youth Institute, October 14, 2014, https://fulleryouthinstitute.org/articles/sticky-faith -and-special-needs.

done. Thoughtful opening sharing questions, attentive empathy to group members throughout, breaking into smaller groups periodically, and involving teenagers in planning and executing your gathering can help young people feel known whether they are sitting shoulder to shoulder or device to device.

Connections through Hospitable Tables

Just because you're sharing a meal doesn't mean teenagers feel like they belong. Whether with one student or a group, try asking the following questions:

- What's your favorite meal? Why do you love it?
- What do you enjoy about eating with other people? What bothers you?
- What makes you feel like you belong at a meal?
- When do you wish you could escape from a meal?

Read this passage from the story of the disciples on the road to Emmaus just after the resurrection: "When he was at the table with them, he took bread, gave thanks, broke it and began to give it to them. Then their eyes were opened and they recognized him, and he disappeared from their sight. They asked each other, 'Were not our hearts burning within us while he talked with us on the road and opened the Scriptures to us?'" (Luke 24:30–32). Then ask:

- What do you think it was like to recognize Jesus when he broke the bread to start eating?
- What do you think it could mean for us to see Jesus when we break bread with one another?
- How does eating together connect us to one another?

Work with teenagers to create some shared ground rules for when you share tables. Start by asking:

- What would make this a safe place to belong and share?
- What are some commitments we want to make to one another about how we're going to eat meals together and talk?

If students have a hard time getting started, here are some examples:

- Everyone is welcome. Everyone belongs at the table.
- We put our phones away (maybe in the same place) before we start.
- We assume the best of each other.
- We ask follow-up questions (such as "Tell me more").
- Everyone gets enough to eat.
- We serve someone else before we serve ourselves.
- Newcomers always sit in between "regulars."

Practice your new ground rules through an actual meal together and debrief what's different and how this way of eating might help with hospitality and belonging.

Connections WITH One Another through Our Stories

This may seem obvious, but sharing and listening to stories are acts of hospitality. Whether one-on-one or in a group setting, take time to exchange stories by asking questions like the following:

- What is one of the earliest stories told about you in your family?

- What's something that happened when you were younger that shaped who you are today?
- How would you describe your family's cultural background, and if your family came to the US from another country at some point or if you have an Indigenous heritage, how does your family talk (or not talk) about those stories?
- Thinking back across your life so far, what stands out about your experience of church and faith? Would

Connection through Tech and Social Media

Teenagers can't always be together—with one another or with adults who matter to them—in person. Nothing elevated this reality like the global pandemic of 2020. Somewhat overnight, adults' anxiety about young people being "constantly on their phones" gave way to relief that "at least they have their phones" to connect with their friends. Digital media and tech began to be seen as part of young people's social safety net.[a]

Pandemic or not, teenagers create spaces of belonging or exclusion on virtual platforms. While these are constantly evolving based on the latest app or game, one of the signifiers of being "in" with a group is being added to some version of a group chat.

For my (Brad's) teenage kids, it's not uncommon to manage multiple group chats across multiple platforms with the same group of friends—and subsets of those groups. It sounds exhausting to me, and it can be. But being part of a group that is messaging one another in a virtual space *is* part of belonging for today's teenagers. And I've seen how being "added to the chat" can make all the difference for new teenagers in our church. It's a way to move from visitor to "one of us."

a. Though similar to other social safety nets, socioeconomics shape access to technology and support in navigating it. Given that one out of two US adolescents lives in poverty or in a low-income household, many young people experience gaps in the digital world. Candice L. Odgers and Michael B. Robb, *Tweens, Teens, Tech, and Mental Health* (San Francisco: Common Sense Media, 2020), 11.

you say you "grew up" in church? What has that been like for you?

- Tell a story about a friend who has been important to you in some way—either someone your age or an adult.

Deeper Connections within Small Groups

It's no secret to youth ministry leaders that small groups play a critical role in connection. But the secrets to great small groups can seem elusive.

Carrie is a youth pastor in a White, high-pressure, affluent Minneapolis suburb who was wrestling with how her students seemed to be stuck in relationally shallow waters. She knew there was much pain hidden under the surface, but the environment in her community pressed pain and struggle down anytime it emerged. Students were barely treading water, and sometimes drowning in despair, but kept up the appearance of perfection—even in their weekly small groups.

Dissatisfied with this pattern, Carrie and her team decided to experiment with small group practices that might reveal more honesty and foster deeper connections. They started by replacing the typical "highs and lows" prompts during small group time with more vulnerable ones. For the first few months, students and adults alike in small groups shared their responses to the following:

If you really knew me, you would know . . .
If I could say anything to God, I would say . . .

The leaders hoped students would engage in more transparent conversations with one another and God as a result.

And they were right. Carrie said, "This practice really helped us break ingrained patterns and open up vulnerability in our small groups."

Whether you are training leaders to be better facilitators or introducing new sharing practices, as Carrie's team did, use the ideas in this chapter to help your small groups become places of deeper belonging.

From Half-Belonging to True Belonging

The story of fitting in is everyone's story. On some level or another, we've all experienced not belonging or only half-belonging. We have felt on the edge of outside, half-included but not really "in."

The season I (Brad) most experienced half-belonging was in middle school. I've already shared in chapter 2 about a teacher who noticed and walked with me during that tough period. Her acceptance was so important because I was experiencing rejection on many other fronts.

I tried a lot of things to fit in. Thankfully, I didn't try anything very harmful; my most desperate attempts were through the channel of fashion. (Feel free to chuckle.)

I belong where I belong. If that needs to be helping people some other place, if that needs to be some other country, if that needs to be across the street, if that needs to be anywhere but where people think I need to be, then that's where I belong. I belong where God feels I need to belong. I belong where God sets me. And I feel like, at the end of the day, I belong where I choose to belong. —Simone

I'll never forget my first Coke shirt. This was a real thing in the late '80s in the South, if nowhere else. The shirt in question was a thick pullover rugby featuring a solid white horizontal stripe across the chest, emblazoned with the red Coca-Cola emblem.

How Coke managed to break into the fashion world remains a mystery, but I sure wanted in on the trend. The kids I hoped to fit in with regularly sported their branded attire at school, and that's all that mattered. I remember trying to figure out how to ask my mom for one of the shirts. She was (and still is) probably the most no-nonsense person I know, so this was no easy feat.

Eventually, I landed one of these prized possessions. I proudly wore it to school at least once a week. That shirt became my marker of belonging. Finally, I had the right clothes to hang out with the cool group. I wanted to feel like these were my friends, that this was where I belonged.

But it also felt like I was just faking it. After all, it wasn't true belonging—it was temporarily fitting in.

Not until later in high school did I really experience belonging in friendships. But I grew to understand that everyone feels that sense of half-belonging sometimes. Maybe much of the time.

Perhaps you too remember begging a parent to buy a particular clothing brand so you could fit in. (For Kara, it was neon T-shirts. She's definitely a by-product of the '80s.) Or maybe it was something else for you—being part of a team, joining a club, or listening to a certain type of music. What you and I really needed to know then and what we need to know now is that regardless of whether we're wearing the right clothes or saying the right things, we belong to God, we are loved, God is WITH us, and we belong WITH God's people.

True belonging starts when we end the tyranny of *just fitting in*, which is really a tyranny of *exclusion*. When our church becomes the kind of community that embodies the bold message of inclusion and belonging, we fulfill this yearning for young people—and all generations.

Christ-Centered Belonging Recap

In this chapter, we provide a handful of summary phrases for you and your teenagers. We've geared these statements to serve not just as a recap but also as reminders of your conversations and connections. Once you have chosen a belonging message you want to remember, the next step is to create a system that reminds you of that truth every day.

You and your young people might want to *set a daily alarm on your phones*—to go off perhaps in the morning as you're getting ready or in the evening as you're winding down—to remind you to think about one or more of these divine truths.

Or maybe go "low tech" and *write God's better message on an index card* you display on your bathroom mirror, car dashboard, or office bookshelf.

Perhaps you and your students can *take turns texting important messages* to each other, strengthening your mutual commitment to being WITH God's people.

Whatever you choose, make sure *you* also do whatever you ask of your young people so you too can share your progress in realizing your true belonging.

Here is a list of messages you can draw from:

- I belong WITH God's people.
- No one belongs here more than I do.
- We are family.
- God is WITH us.
- We are known by our love.
- We are the body of Christ.
- I belong everywhere because I belong to God.
- Hospitality means giving the privileges of insiders to outsiders.
- True belonging starts when we end the tyranny of just fitting in.

REFLECT and APPLY

1. Which of the conversation or hospitality connection ideas in this chapter would be best for you and the young people you know?

2. What difference might that conversation or connection make in you and in your young people's sense of belonging?

3. What might you and your young people have to adjust in your relationships or routines to make time for that change? What would make it worthwhile to make that change?

4. What prayer would you like to offer as you help young people, as well as yourself, understand that we belong WITH God's people?

PART IV

WHAT
DIFFERENCE
CAN I MAKE?

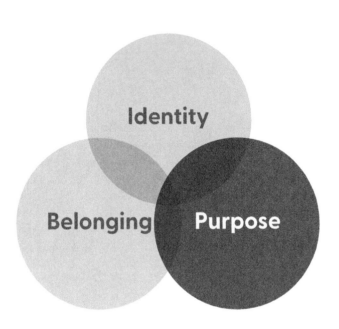

The Big Question of Purpose

My main purpose is to be nice to other people. That makes people like me more. It makes everything easier for me, because everybody loves a nice guy.

Leo

Rebekah decided, "I want to be known as someone who cares. Even when it is really, really, *really* difficult, I want to be viewed as somebody who loves well."

Until the faculty at Rebekah's private Christian school asked her senior class to think about their legacy, she hadn't thought about it much. But thanks to Rebekah's confident personality and leadership skills, she had been weaving a web of caring relationships for years.

As a member of her youth group's leadership team, Rebekah has stepped forward to be an example at church and school. Last month that meant the bold leap of sharing her testimony with a few hundred students at Wednesday night youth group. When asked how that felt, Rebekah replied with characteristic zeal: "It was fun! It was good. I was freaking out!"

After high school graduation, Rebekah wants to be a youth ministry summer intern so she can learn the ins and outs of church leadership. Since Rebekah's birth, her mom and dad have insisted on bringing her and her younger brother to church. Now that Rebekah can drive herself, her parents sometimes don't make it to Sunday worship. But Rebekah's there—multiple times every week.

Part of what magnetically draws Rebekah to church even when her parents skip is her small group. Since sixth grade, she's been devoted to the weekly group, composed mostly of girls who also attend her school. In addition to being together in small group, the girls stay in touch by text, "reminding ourselves every day that we cannot do it on our own."

The girls' commitment to one another peaked in the fall of eleventh grade when the mom of one of Rebekah's closest friends was diagnosed with terminal cancer. Rebekah tried to support Allison and her family however she could, spending lots of afternoons and evenings at Allison's house.

Allison's mom passed away in February, raising new faith questions for Rebekah. According to Rebekah, "It was the first time that someone I cared about went through something that didn't turn out okay in the end." She recounted how those "long months really challenged my relationship with the Lord."

It wasn't until summer camp that Rebekah could admit to her youth pastor that she was furious at God for letting Allison's mom die. A year later, Rebekah still doesn't understand why God didn't heal her. But she's now realizing that "God wasn't punishing me, Allison, or her family. I've learned a lot about grace and trusting that God is still good even when things suck."

Senior year highlights that Allison and Rebekah share—without Allison's mom—are bittersweet. Allison was selected by the student body to be homecoming queen. In the midst of that thrill, she confided in Rebekah, "I really wish my mom was here."

Rebekah is close to her own mom. "When my mom hears what I'm going through, she says, 'I get it, I hear how you feel, that makes sense.'" Inspired by her mom's empathy and her small group leader's career as a therapist, Rebekah wants to be a counselor. In large part thanks to her faith community, Rebekah's pretty good at connecting the dots between who she is, what she's invested in, and the impact she wants to have on others.

Defining Purpose: What Difference Can I Make?

Our purpose is *our contribution to the world*. Like a compass pointing north, purpose provides Rebekah and each of us—at any age—life direction.[1] Despite the value of this orientation, it's estimated that four out of ten Americans have not yet discovered a satisfying life purpose.[2]

Our understanding of our purpose evolves over our lifetime, with adolescence and young adulthood often being seasons of escalating clarity. Sometimes that clarity comes from resolving the tension of seeing unlimited roads to the future while simultaneously feeling pressured to follow specific lanes prescribed to help one "get into a good college" or "find the right job." Other times increased certainty comes as

As we've seen already, the 3 big questions of identity, belonging, and purpose constantly reflect and reinforce one another. In fact, multiple studies confirm that feeling a sense of belonging is an important prerequisite to discovering purpose.[a] Our interviewees who expressed their purpose through social activism seemed to enjoy doing it *with others*—thus filling their hunger for both purpose and belonging.

And yet the 3 big questions have distinct functions and goals. For instance, while identity is focused on *who* I want to become, purpose attends to *what* I hope to achieve.[b]

young people finally figure out what they are good at, after years of knowing only what they aren't.

Regardless of age or the degree of clarity, purpose unites two (sometimes divergent) interests—what's worthwhile *to us* as well as what's consequential for the world *around us*.[3] Put simply, purpose is meaningful both for us and beyond us.[4]

Four Current Answers for Purpose: I Make a Difference . . .

The best research on purpose, as well as our national interviews with churched teenagers, highlights four dominant answers to the big question "What difference can I make?"

I Make a Difference When I'm Helping Others

> I make a difference when I'm caring for others, making them feel good and happy, being a hero—when someone is depending on me.

Across our discussions about identity, belonging, and purpose, youth group students felt a universal impulse to help

---

a. Kendall Cotton Bronk, *Purpose in Life: A Critical Component of Optimal Youth Development* (Dordrecht, Netherlands: Springer Science & Business Media, 2014), 118.
b. Bronk, *Purpose in Life*, 72.

> *I want to make a difference in people's lives, not necessarily like a big world-changing type of thing, but so that people will think, "Oh, wow, that was kind, or that was cool for her to do." —Sue*

others. Every single teenager we met with talked about "helping" at least once during our three interviews with them. In fact, they talked about service and helping others more than any other path to purpose.

In his Boy Scout troop, church, and family, Steve desired to "help as many people in as many ways as I can. . . . Whether it is talking to someone who needs to get something off their chest or helping someone move stuff out of their house, I find purpose any time and any place I can help someone else."

Arthur described those moments when he feels he's doing what he is meant to do: "It's when I'm teaching people. I never feel stressed when somebody at school comes to me for help learning music or math they can't grasp on their own."

Helping through Social Activism

Having encountered the failing prospects of the so-called "American Dream," Stanford anthropologist Roberta Katz concluded that today's young people "know they are confronting a future of big challenges—not just whether they can find jobs or own homes, but how they will handle climate change, artificial intelligence, genetic engineering, 3-D-printed guns, and pandemic illnesses—and, depending on the person, are afraid, resigned, or energized."[5] (Katz didn't realize how prophetic she was in warning about "pandemic illnesses" just months prior to a worldwide outbreak's arrival in the US.)

Afraid. Resigned. Energized. We saw all three responses, but much more of the latter.

Race-focused activism sparked energy among these students. One high school senior we interviewed was planning to develop workshops for his diverse youth group on racial reconciliation. We mentioned in chapter 2 that Janelle serves as a leader in her school's Black Student Union. In that role, she spearheaded a campaign on African American mental health struggles.

Caring for our planet was also on teenagers' minds in our interviews. When asked what she and other teenagers are worried about, Lilly responded, "I think climate change is a big one. It's kind of ironic because here I am drinking out of a plastic cup even as I say that. But it's important to reduce waste or recycle properly and be more mindful of our planet's natural resources."

Daniel is a junior who answered that question even more personally. Having experienced homelessness for a year when his dad was ill and unable to work, Daniel is mindful of the kids who are homeless in his neighborhood. He rattled off the effects of homelessness—ranging from pollution to crime—that he had seen and encountered himself. Now that Daniel's family can afford an apartment, he's raising money to help those who are homeless, picking up trash to keep the streets cleaner, and advocating with city officials for more homeless shelters.

The Positive and Negative Effects of Helping Others

Young people who channel their resources and skills to benefit others tend to have higher rates of happiness and well-being.[6] Time and time again, students like Rebekah, Lilly, and Daniel described feeling better when they help others. Natalie lit up when describing how creating care packages for the homeless in her community makes her feel: "It really shows me that I am a loving person, no matter what anyone says about me. Down in my core, down in my heart, I am a kind person."

For Claudia, college application essay questions have crystallized her desire to boldly pursue a future career in journalism. She looks ahead to knowing "I am fulfilling my purpose when I wake up every day and am happy to go to my job because I know what I'm doing helps other people."

While most teenagers who described helping others gave similarly glowing reports, our guess is that about one-third of those same young people were potentially serving so much that their own health suffered. When asked to describe her favorite video personality or character on a show, Sofia described relating to Clay from the controversial Netflix series *13 Reasons Why*: "He is always trying to help others, and he doesn't really pay attention to himself. I identify with him because I am always doing stuff for other people and don't really take care of myself."

Lilly was even more specific in chronicling the cost of serving others: "My physical, mental, and emotional health sometimes suffer when I try to make others happy. As their

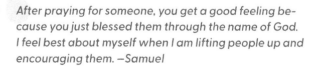

After praying for someone, you get a good feeling because you just blessed them through the name of God. I feel best about myself when I am lifting people up and encouraging them. —Samuel

happiness increases, mine sometimes deteriorates. But it's like, I still want to keep helping, so I do."

In his role as a part-time church intern, Sebastian tries to be on top of details so other leaders don't feel anxious. "I have to make sure that the pastor is fine and that she doesn't have to worry about anything. My goal is to allow everyone else to rely on me, so she doesn't have to worry about anything on stage."

In his focus on helping other leaders and congregants, Sebastian is often at church on Sundays from 7 a.m. to 9 p.m. but gets little time with his church friends. "I sort of stay in the sound booth in the back, so I don't really interact with people at church. Sometimes friends will stop by in the back and say, 'Hey, how are you?' But I can't really answer because I'm focused on doing the tech stuff and keeping things running."

Experiencing Purpose Personally

After pastoring in two large church plants in youth, college, and family ministries, Jane Hong-Guzmán de León now influences youth leaders across the country as an FYI team member. Given her background and diverse life experiences, Jane offers insights into the intersection between ethnicity and purpose as well as how adults can help young people unwrap their God-given gifts for our world.

> KARA: Jane, how did you define your sense of purpose when you were a teenager?

> JANE: I have felt God's presence strongly in my life since I was saved in junior high, and wanting to help people has always been part of my journey. As a teenager, a friend shared with me how she had been cutting herself because of her emotional pain. I wanted to help but I didn't know

how. My church offered a great youth program, but the answers they gave didn't always match the questions we were asking. That was hard for me because I wanted my life to have meaning and I found a deep sense of purpose in helping others. So I ended up asking God deeper questions about pain and difficulties and looking for ways we could equip ourselves to partner with God toward healing and transformation.

KARA: You were part of a Korean American church as a young person. How did that church affect your sense of purpose?

JANE: My sense of purpose was initially very much shaped by my church's communal way of looking at life. Culturally, we gather and do life together as if we're family. Meals, needs, hardships, and celebrations—we share everything and sacrifice for one another within the church. When we think of doing things for God, we do it together as a church.

I've also experienced the power of prayer and having grit in your faith because I saw how first-generation immigrants like my parents kept pushing forward. In Korean churches, we understand that suffering is part of our faith journey, and we find strength together in God's greater purpose for our lives.

But one challenge in figuring out purpose in such a communal setting is that I lacked opportunities to figure out the unique ways God could use *me* outside of doing church together. So it took more time and intentionality to discover my sense of purpose as an individual.

KARA: What have you learned about purpose by interviewing teenagers?

JANE: I am reminded that youth need to be invited to experience God and tangibly be part of the body. Teenagers can't learn to have a vibrant faith by just listening to adults and talking about it. They have to experience it. They need to pray for others and experience doing ministry themselves. Adults have lived longer and can sometimes see the potential and possibilities young people can't yet see. Teenagers need adults who take the time to get to know them, asking, "You know those passions that you have? I bet God put those in your heart for a reason. What would it look like to develop them further?"

I Make a Difference When I Follow the Script

I make a difference when I've been given clear roles and lines and I follow them, when I know the right things to do (mostly things my family or church says), when I do what I'm supposed to do.

While not as frequent as "helping others," a second answer teenagers gave to the big question of purpose was following the roles and lines handed them by others. Given all the possible routes ahead of them, our interviewees seemed fine, and often almost eager, to be assigned a lane by the explicit or implicit "rules" of their friends, family, or faith community. Despite interviewees' desire to express some individuality, in a world of endless options, they appreciated ready-made highways.

While academic pressures cut across ethnicity and backgrounds, students from families that more recently immigrated often feel heightened pressure because of sacrifices made to move to the US. Claudia is grateful to her mom for leaving academic possibilities behind in Mexico and knows it's extra important that she now seizes educational opportunities of her own. "My mom says that even though her academic career wasn't fulfilled, at least her children are going to have a better future and education."

In some homes, the family script also mandates taking care of younger siblings. Sofia rushes home from school on weekdays so she can care for her little sister and help with housework. Sofia recalled, "As soon as my little sister was born, my mom went back to work. It was hard enough to watch my sister as a baby. It got even harder when she was two years old and started putting everything in her mouth. I really had to watch her then."

Predictably, given that every teenager we interviewed was nominated by a youth pastor or church leader, these rules include assumptions about faith and faith community. Multiple students described their faith transitioning from an external script imposed by others to an internal script they were drafting themselves. Having grown up on a steady diet of church, Rebekah and her friends often get "bored" with the gospel when it's "all you've been fed all the time since childhood." After Rebekah worked through the death of her friend's mom, her faith became more personal to her. "I realized I had to choose for myself about my relationship with the Lord. I could not just keep going through the motions with a faith that was not my own. I literally couldn't keep doing it anymore."

Teenagers' efforts to discover God's plan for their future seem to generate both peace and pressure. Lilly nervously admitted, "I have a career in mind that I want to do, but I don't know if that's what God wants for me. What if I pursue it and it ends up not being God's best for me? I will have spent four years studying something only to scrap it and start all over. I keep changing my mind about what I want to be. I'm wondering how many times it will change before I finally land on what God wants me to do."

Much of Lilly's anxiety about missing God's plan for her life stems from the well-intentioned but stress-laden teachings of her former middle school pastor. "He really emphasized knowing God's vision for us. Ever since then, I've been tripped up about different paths I'm interested in, wondering which is God's vision for me. I have always been told that our purpose as humans is to advance God's kingdom, and I want to do that. But I'm stressed because I don't know *how* I'm supposed to do that."

The pressure to have a clear sense of their future, whether connected or not with God's plan for them, was mentioned by one-third of the students we interviewed and by most seniors. Michael from the upper Midwest "feels like a failure" because "this time of year everyone talks about what they are going to do. And it feels like everyone else knows exactly what they're going to do. Not knowing makes you feel out of it and different."

I Make a Difference When I Get to Make Choices about My Life

> I make a difference when I feel like I have agency and power to choose at least some of what happens in my life.

While the young people we interviewed were surprisingly unresentful about the scripts handed to them, their third path to purpose came from sensing they could choose (at least some of) what happens in their lives. They wanted, and appreciated, having a sense of agency—the opportunity to develop their own interests, goals, and values.[7]

Seemingly less driven by tangible rewards or public recognition, today's students want to make their own decisions. And they hope those decisions will shape our world.[8]

The year Daniel's family struggled with housing, they were never on the streets. Thanks to his mom's creative planning, Daniel and his family lived out of suitcases and slept in friends' family rooms, thereby avoiding the plight of so many in similar circumstances. That proactivity instilled in

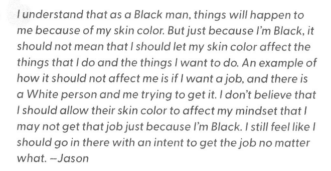

I understand that as a Black man, things will happen to me because of my skin color. But just because I'm Black, it should not mean that I should let my skin color affect the things that I do and the things I want to do. An example of how it should not affect me is if I want a job, and there is a White person and me trying to get it. I don't believe that I should allow their skin color to affect my mindset that I may not get that job just because I'm Black. I still feel like I should go in there with an intent to get the job no matter what. —Jason

Daniel a survival instinct that translates into a commitment to plan for his own future. He fervently explained, "I try not to hang around people who are lazy or not doing their work. They don't see a future for themselves. I've always had a dream for my future. I want to be a scientist who discovers something and helps change the world. Like maybe invent the next Google or something. I want to do something fun, but also something that matters."

Unlike Daniel, who is single-minded in his pursuit of one career, many students we met were more like Claudia, who wants the freedom to change her plans—multiple times. She humorously detailed how she initially wanted to be a vet: "But then I saw a documentary about a lady who died because this cat with a virus in its claw scratched her. I was like, 'No, I am not trying to die.' So then I was interested in being a lawyer, but the law changes every week. So no, that's not it. Then I realized I like to read and write and talk about what's going on in the world, so I thought I could pursue creative writing and journalism. That way I can motivate people to take action, like with the burning of the Amazon rainforest. So now that's what I want to do."

The young people we interviewed took pride not just in choosing their own worthwhile work but also in the tangible signs of trust and respect bestowed on them by adults. Sebastian is proud of the responsibilities his church assigns him. "My church gives me tasks that they wouldn't give to most seventeen-year-olds. I have the security code for our building. I have the key. I am in charge of offering on the weekends. That is pretty big. When people at my church entrust me to do things at such a great level, I feel like I belong. And like my life has meaning."

I Make a Difference When I'm Headed toward a Good Future

> I make a difference when I'm building a good future for me and others I care about, when I'm achieving, excelling, and moving toward what I define as "the good life," when I'm being my best self.

The future of our world is bleak, but my future is bright. That's the essence of the "optimism gap" documented by student researcher Sophia Pink after driving across the US interviewing twenty-one-year-olds. They used words such as "scary," "destruction," and "dumpster fire" to describe what's forthcoming for America. But when the same young people imagine their own futures, responses ranged from "hopeful" to "determined" and "loving."[9] In FYI's analysis of 2,092 young people, we also saw a bias toward describing their own lives and futures positively.

The self-optimism of these twenty-one-year-olds aligns with the fourth current answer that emerged from our inter-

About two-thirds of fifteen- to twenty-one-year-olds feel very or somewhat significantly stressed about our nation's future (68 percent) and do not believe the US is moving toward being stronger than ever (66 percent).[a]

view questions about purpose. While the exact target was murky and varied with each teenager, the majority of our youth group kids were aiming toward their conception of "the good life."

For many of the students we interviewed, that target includes three circles: faith, financial success, and fulfillment. In talking about the future he's working toward, Michael said he wants to be like his dad and "find a job that I can succeed at. And that I like doing so I don't mind going to work. I'm willing to work hard but I want to find a job I enjoy. I want my employees to talk about what a good guy I am. When something goes wrong, I want to show that I'm different because of my faith."

Natalie feels drawn to an acting career but will likely choose a different profession that provides the financial stability she desires. This ninth grader finds the field of healthcare appealing because she can "make the world a better place and still be financially stable. If you're more financially stable, I feel like you are more likely to make the world a better place. That's just kind of how our country works."

While most students viewed their best future as a brew of financial prosperity and personal fulfillment, a handful distilled theirs to personal relationships. As a senior about to graduate, Arthur treasures close relationships above all

a. American Psychological Association, "Stress in America: Generation Z," October 2018, 3, https://www.apa .org/news/press/releases/stress/2018/stress-gen-z.pdf.

The research of Yale scholar Almeda Wright, an advisor for this project, highlights how visions of the future can differ across racial demographics. She notes, "Death, violence, oppression, and racism have become part of the narratives of all young African Americans, whether they are experiencing these firsthand or just reading about them on social media. Parents and youth workers are also struggling and wondering how to walk with young people in a world such as this. For some youth, there is not a longing for a brighter future; rather, they simply wonder if they will get a chance to grow up and if they will be alive."[a]

else: "You cannot have everything. I want to be satisfied with what I have and able to appreciate those who love and surround me. Most people define happiness as having everything you want, but sometimes that still feels empty. For me, being able to love everybody in my life is the best happiness."

Even more succinctly, Lilly defined her "happy life" in one sentence: "Being content with God and what God has given me, and learning to be faithful rather than complain."

Whatever their picture of a "good future," churched kids are working hard to make that image their reality. Often too hard. Sebastian spends so many hours volunteering at church that others tell him, "You should enjoy yourself and go hang out with your friends." Sebastian admitted, "They're right that I'm probably too focused on achieving my future goals to become a youth pastor. I'm trying to remember to enjoy the time I have now instead of always striving and pushing myself harder."

a. Almeda M. Wright, *The Spiritual Lives of Young African Americans* (New York: Oxford University Press, 2017), 198.

Big Question	Focus	Description	Current Answers	Christ-Centered Answer
Who am I?	Identity	Our view of ourselves	*I am...* • what others expect. • not _____ enough. • my image. • more than my label.	I'm ENOUGH because of Jesus.
Where do I fit?	Belonging	Our connection with others	*I fit...* • where I feel safe to be me. • where we share _____. • where I feel like I'm needed.	I belong WITH God's people.
What difference can I make?	Purpose	Our contribution to the world	*I make a difference...* • when I'm helping others. • when I follow the script. • when I get to make choices about my life. • when I'm headed toward a good future.	

Clear but Still Lacking

Of the 3 big questions that change teenagers, our interviewees had more coherent descriptions of their purpose than their identity or belonging. Our hunch is that since students are handed specific scripts from family, friends, teachers, mentors, and pastors about their expected gift to the world, they find it easier to repeat back those lines.

While our interviewees certainly had clear intentions to shape our world, their plans still often felt a little bit flat.

Two-dimensional.

Somewhat gray and bland.

As we'll explore in the next chapter, they often lacked the vividness that comes from Christ's full-color vision of being changed by grace to change our world.

REFLECT and APPLY

1. Below are the four current answers young people commonly use to define their purpose. To help you empathize with today's teenagers, reflect on yourself as a teenager. Rank the answers on a scale of 1 to 4, giving a 1 to the answer that was most common for you and a 4 to the one you identified with least.

          "I make a difference when I'm helping others."

          "I make a difference when I follow the script."

          "I make a difference when I get to make choices about my life."

          "I make a difference when I'm headed toward a good future."

2. Looking back, what was helpful about the answers you gravitated toward?

3. What was perhaps hurtful to you or others?

4. Now think about a young person you know and repeat the same process, placing a 1 next to their most common purpose answer and a 4 next to their least common purpose answer.

        "I make a difference when I'm helping others."

        "I make a difference when I follow the script."

        "I make a difference when I get to make choices about my life."

        "I make a difference when I'm headed toward a good future."

5. What about their top two current answers is helpful?

6. What is perhaps harmful about them?

7. Two of the themes that cut across all four answers are that young people are working hard to find purpose and that uncertainty about their future makes them anxious. How are one, or both, of those themes true of the young people you care about most?

8. In the next chapter, we will explore a better Christ-centered answer to our longing for purpose. Without looking ahead (no cheating!), what ideas do you already have for Jesus' better answer to our big question of purpose?

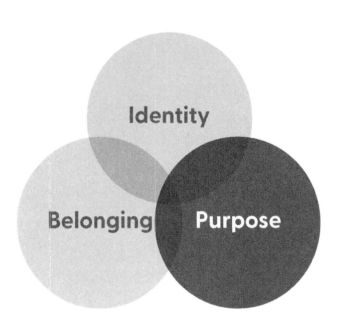

STORY:
Jesus' Better Answer

I think of myself like a pencil. I can try to be a utensil to eat with—like a fork or a chopstick—but that's not my purpose. Either I'm writing and being used for God's purposes or I'm not.

Kevin

The church is a theatre of the gospel in which disciples stage previews of the coming kingdom of God.

Kevin J. Vanhoozer[1]

So yeah, I'm deeply involved at my church now. I feel like I'm part of the family. I have a mission, and purpose, identity, belonging. All the stuff that teens generally want."

When Kevin, a biracial high school senior, mentioned "purpose, identity, belonging" in our initial interview—even before I (Kara) did—I was impressed.

I couldn't resist going off script and asking, "Kevin, you just mentioned *identity*, *belonging*, and *purpose*. Much of the rest of the interview is about those three terms. I'm curious: Have you heard these words before?"

Chuckling, Kevin smiled and admitted, "You busted me. I actually googled you and the Fuller Youth Institute last night and watched some of your videos."

That's not quite as astounding as coming up with those three terms on his own, but it's still extraordinary. Kevin was the only student we interviewed who went online to study us before we studied him.

Kevin's intentionality in looking up the Fuller Youth Institute mirrors the intentionality with which he's experimented with his purpose for the last half of high school. A couple of years ago, Kevin launched his own YouTube channel to draw viewers to Jesus. He clarified, "I don't make videos. But I've compiled, like, hundreds of videos and blogs that are the most helpful and popular when it comes to philosophy, ethics, morality, and stuff like that."

In college and beyond, Kevin wants to write accessible and provocative content that points other teenagers to Jesus' life and teachings. "Have you read *Diary of a Wimpy Kid*? I'd like to write like that. Nonchalant. Kind of cool. Maybe with drawings. But through the lens of the church. For people my age."

A month before our first meeting, Kevin was hired on staff at his church. He's now paid to supervise the (mostly adult) weekend volunteers as they set up chairs and tables in their main meeting spaces.

While the church pays him a small stipend, Kevin's more motivated by his dreams for his church's impact. "I think of church like a spiritual hospital to heal those in need. And like a spiritual military base to reach those who are lost. Youth group should be where we are equipped and held accountable as we go throughout the week." Talking with this seventeen-year-old often felt like having a conversation with a twenty-seven-year-old—a twenty-seven-year-old with a remarkably clear vision for the part he plays in God's kingdom work. He views himself as an agent in God's bigger plan and "part of the greatest story ever told, meaning the gospel. I'm always asking myself, 'How is my story going to further God's plot? Where does the writer, who is God, need my character?' I'm not the main character, but I serve the main character, who is Jesus."

The Christ-Centered Answer in One Word: STORY

Like Kevin, our team believes Christ-centered purpose comes from knowing we're invited into God's greater STORY.

> *You are a novel.* You are an extended prose narrative featuring a main character.
>
> Dan P. McAdams[2]

Our lives don't become meaningful because we're helping others.

Or following the right rules.

Or making our own choices to pursue "the good life."

Our best answer to the question "What difference can I make?" is that our lives matter because we are part of the ongoing plot of what God has done, is doing, and will do in our world.

We're surrounded by stories that want to claim our attention and direct our purpose. In *After Virtue*, Scottish philosopher Alasdair MacIntyre asserts, "I cannot answer

Our life stories are shaped by who we are and where we are headed, thus creating yet another junction between the big questions of identity and purpose.

In addition, since those most influential in our lives become characters in our stories, our relationships help form our stories. Daniel Taylor highlights this intersection between belonging and purpose:

> No one's story exists alone. Each is tangled up in countless others. Pull a thread in my story and feel the tremor half a world and two millennia away.[a]

the question, 'What ought I to do?' unless I first answer the question, 'Of which story am I a part?'"[3]

That may be the most important sentence in this chapter.

Our contribution to the world is contingent on whose story we make central in our lives.

Imagine three teenagers, each centered on a different narrative, responding to the extended social distancing required during a pandemic. Tenth-grade Colin revolves his story around his friends and passion for baseball, so an extended separation from both could cause panic. Eleventh-grade Audrey centers her story around her family, so she feels greater peace knowing being home will fill her tank. Eduardo is a senior whose primary narrative is an urgency to help others, so he works virtually from his bedroom to mobilize friends and family to meet neighbors' quarantine needs.

None of these are terrible core stories. Friends, family, and the needs of others are worthy sources of purpose, right?

Absolutely.

But they can easily miss the full-fledged purpose that comes from making God's STORY our central life story. Friends are flawed and will let us down. Our families can be

a. Daniel Taylor, *Tell Me a Story: The Life-Shaping Power of Our Stories* (St. Paul: Bog Walk Press, 2001), 6.

great but will never be perfect. Our neighbors will thank us but never love us unconditionally.

Our best personal narratives come from embedding our stories in the ultimate narrative of God's STORY. Each of us finds our utmost meaning and purpose as a supporting character whose life revolves around God, Jesus, and the Holy Spirit as the authors and main characters. As the late pastor, theologian, and poet Eugene Peterson celebrated, "God is the larger context and plot in which our stories find themselves."[4] Or in the words of the book of Hebrews, Jesus is the "author and perfecter of our faith" (12:2 ASV).

We're Invited into God's Greater STORY: 1 Corinthians 3:5–9

While God could unfold this divine STORY without us, he chooses not to. We humans are not invisible extras wandering aimlessly behind the scenes. As we learn from the apostle Paul's insights in 1 Corinthians 3:5–9, it's God's drama, but we and young people can play a vital part today.

God's STORY Is the Bigger Story

The city of Corinth was full of citizens who wanted to move up financially and socially, often by aligning themselves with a particular local leader or celebrity. Even followers of Christ were choosing teams.[5]

Paul fights these cultural norms and cuts his followers' ties to himself and another well-known leader, Apollos, by writing, "What, after all, is Apollos? And what is Paul? Only servants, through whom you came to believe" (1 Cor. 3:5). Resisting the gravitational pull of human allegiance common in his readers, Paul points instead to the One who set the universe in motion.

Paul builds on this theme of God's centrality through agrarian metaphors familiar to the Corinthians: "I planted the seed, Apollos watered it, but God has been making it grow. So neither the one who plants nor the one who waters is anything, but only God, who makes things grow. The one who plants and the one who waters have one purpose, and they will each be rewarded according to their own labor. For we are co-workers in God's service; you are God's field, God's building" (vv. 6–9).

To first-century farmers who felt ever susceptible to weather and natural forces they couldn't influence, Paul proclaims that it is God who makes all things grow. The verb tense for *grow* actually means "keeps it growing." The Holy Spirit's ongoing work brought growth yesterday, brings growth today, and will bring growth tomorrow. Paul and Apollos have the honor of being called "co-workers in God's service," but all credit for the fruit of that work goes to God.

Defining God's STORY and Playing Our Part

Brad and I like to view Scripture as describing five-sixths of God's divine drama.[6] We know the history that's come before us: creation, fall, covenant, and Jesus compose acts 1–4. The hints we're given about Christ's return and the new creation to come look ahead to act 6.[7]

But then there's a portion that we help create. Act 5 is partially missing. Empowered by the Holy Spirit, the New Testament church put the first part of this act into motion. The same Holy Spirit works in and through Christ followers today. What we live out now—every day as God's people—is the second part of the act. That's why we like thinking of discipleship as our everyday "Yes" to Jesus.

When Kevin shares his faith online, he's improvising in the fifth act of God's unfolding drama. When he mobilizes volunteers at his church, he's reenacting God's STORY, making it more tangible. He's being a disciple.

God knits together Kevin's discipleship with the rest of our stories and creates one grand narrative. Later in 1 Corinthians, Paul describes the power of threading our stories together this way: "There are different kinds of gifts, but the same Spirit distributes them. There are different kinds of service, but the same Lord. There are different kinds of working, but in all of them and in everyone it is the same God at work" (12:4–6).

In other words, in this drama, everyone has a part to play.

Big Question	Focus	Description	Current Answers	Christ-Centered Answer
Who am I?	Identity	Our view of ourselves	*I am...* • what others expect. • not _____ enough. • my image. • more than my label.	I'm ENOUGH because of Jesus.
Where do I fit?	Belonging	Our connection with others	*I fit...* • where I feel safe to be me. • where we share _____. • where I feel like I'm needed.	I belong WITH God's people.
What difference can I make?	Purpose	Our contribution to the world	*I make a difference...* • when I'm helping others. • when I follow the script. • when I get to make choices about my life. • when I'm headed toward a good future.	I'm invited into God's greater STORY.

STORY Gets Practical—Conversations and Connections

Maybe because theater was so important to me (Brad) in middle and high school while I explored the 3 big questions, I'm drawn to the simple idea of being *caught up in God's STORY*. I like it so much that we use the phrase every week in our church's worship service when we send children and middle schoolers into age-group programs: "May the Holy Spirit open our hearts as we are caught up in God's story today."

Christian ethicist Samuel Wells writes, "When a person enters the scriptural story, he or she does so by entering the Church's performance of that story. . . . It is not so much being written into a book as taking part in a play."[8]

By being part of a community that practices God's STORY, it becomes less of a fairy tale and more of a daily reality.

That's one of a host of reasons that our conversations and connections with young people matter. Every day, every week, through the ideas in the rest of this chapter that you talk about and try, you help young people discover and rehearse their part in God's STORY.

Conversations about Purpose

A Conversation about Your Story

The following questions about story, largely from our interview protocols,[9] are best raised with teenagers not in one sitting but over multiple conversations.

NOW

1. Sometimes people might think about their life as a book with different chapters. If you or someone else

wanted to write a book about your life so far, how would you break it up into chapters?

2. Which chapter stands out the most to you, perhaps because it's important in some way?

3. If you were to describe your life story in a few adjectives, what would they be?

4. What words would you use to describe yourself as a character in your story currently?

5. Who are other important characters in your story? What role(s) do they play?

GOD

6. What part does God play in your story—a leading role, a director, or an extra?

7. What part would you like God to play in your story? I wonder why you'd choose that role?

HOW

8. What qualities do you wish were truer of your life story?

9. In whose story have you been an important character? What actions can you take to make their story even better?

10. What would you like to be said about your life by those who know you? How might that impact your decisions?

A Conversation about God's STORY

To help you and your young people further discuss whether God is a main character or an extra in the background in your stories, unpack the following questions.

NOW

1. How would you describe God to a friend? Do you have a particular image or description you associate with God?

2. How much would you say God is part of the way you see your story now? On a scale of 1 to 10, with 1 being "not much" and 10 being "completely," how much does your faith permeate your story?

GOD

3. Is there a story about God that sort of says it all for you?

4. If you had to describe God's overall STORY, or the gospel, what would you say? (You can share the examples earlier in the chapter of God's STORY as a six-act drama to spark their thinking. Ask them which aspects of those examples they like and what they might tweak, change, cut, or add.)

5. Which passages of Scripture seem especially important to your view of God and God's STORY?

HOW

6. What do you *no longer* believe about God's STORY that you used to believe?

> *I write a lot of songs for other people. I write songs based on what I see. One time I spent a whole entire day writing a song for my friend. I wrote the lyrics to cheer her up. When I played it for her, she cried. That was one of the moments that I was like "Okay, I can see myself doing this. I can see myself writing songs for other people," and that feels really good. —Simone*

7. What do you *now* believe about God's STORY that you didn't used to believe?

A Conversation about Your Superpower

Some of the best conversations about purpose help young people unwrap, and then offer, their unique gifts—or

---

Here's my (Kara's) favorite brief description of God's STORY. Part of why I have adopted this version is that it's simple and memorable. Eleven-year-olds can grasp these five key words that start with the letter G.[a] (Note from Brad: You'll see that Kara's version of God's STORY seems more like a list. Having worked with Kara for fifteen years, I can affirm that Kara *really* likes lists.)

GOOD: The first G word is *good*. All of us are created good, in God's image.

GUILT: The second G is *guilt*. Our sin leaves us estranged from God.

GRACE: By God's *grace*, God sent Jesus to be crucified and resurrected so we can be restored. Our repentance offers real life in the present as well as eternal life with God.

GOD'S PEOPLE: As we experience adoption into the body of Christ, we embody God's reign in the world. We are part of the *people of God* joining in the mission and work of God as exemplified in the life and teachings of Christ.

GRATITUDE: The final G word helps connect the dots between the previous four Gs and the commands of Scripture.[b] Why do we try to obey what God has instructed us to do? It's not to make God love or like us more. It's not to feel better about ourselves.

It's because we're so full of *gratitude*. As Dave and I have tried to teach our three teenagers, our lives become great big thank-you notes back to God for all he has done for us.

---

a. Adapted from Kara E. Powell, *The Sticky Faith Guide for Your Family* (Grand Rapids: Zondervan, 2014), 46–47. A true narrative theologian would probably cringe at the way I've distilled God's STORY into principles, let alone that all start with the same letter. My pragmatic interest in offering young people a version of the gospel that is both clear and memorable is what draws me to this paradigm.

b. "Gratitude, though, is more than a mental exercise, more than a formula of words. . . . To be grateful is to recognize the Love of God in everything He has given us—and He has given us everything. *Every breath we draw is a gift of His love, every moment of existence is a grace*, for it brings with it immense graces from Him. Gratitude therefore takes nothing for granted, is never unresponsive, is constantly awakening to new wonder and to praise of the goodness of God. For the grateful man [sic] knows that God is good, not by hearsay but by experience. And that is what makes all the difference." Thomas Merton, *Thoughts in Solitude* (New York: Farrar, Straus & Giroux, 1999), 20, emphasis original.

superpowers—given by the Holy Spirit. Whether your nearest teenagers are crystal clear or fairly murky about their superpower, try discussing the following questions.

NOW

1. What do you like or love to do?
2. When do you feel most alive?
3. What gifts or talents do others see in you?

GOD

4. What are you normally doing in those moments when you feel most connected to others?
5. What are you doing in those moments when you feel closest to God?

HOW

6. What are you interested in doing in the future?
7. How can you get some practice in those interests?

A Conversation Exploring Vocation

Whether in a one-on-one discussion with a teenager or with a group of students, center this discussion on one student (other students will get their turn later). Ask that one student to write down their skills, and you (and anyone else with you) also write down skills and talents you see in that young person.

Then ask the student being highlighted to draft a second list of the causes, issues, or ideas they are passionate about, and you (and anyone else with you) also write down passions you see in them.

When you are finished, write the words "God's STORY" on a bigger sheet of paper or a whiteboard and make two

In the last decade, movies and shows popular with teenage audiences have often centered on superheroes. These characters are constantly rewriting narratives—of their own lives as well as of our world. In these stories, teen and adult superheroes are navigating questions of identity, belonging, and purpose, which is part of the reason they are so appealing to young people. These characters reinforce the message that you get more than one chance to figure out your gifts and the ways to use—or misuse—them in the world.[a]

You've perhaps heard of Greta Thunberg, a Swedish teenager who tapped into her superpower on a global stage. For nearly a year, she staged a mostly solitary climate strike outside Parliament, demanding change for the sake of her generation's life and health. Social media exploded in fall 2019 when she spoke to the United Nations, and something like four million young people joined in protests globally. She was met with plenty of backlash, mostly from adults, and in response she chose to elevate part of her story that might not have been an obvious asset: she lives with Asperger's syndrome.

Thunberg wrote on social media, "When haters go after your looks and differences, it means they have nowhere left to go. And then you know you're winning! I have Asperger's and that means I'm sometimes a bit different from the norm. And—given the right circumstances—being different is a superpower."

Like a character out of a Marvel movie, Greta is working to rewrite the story she's been given by the world.

columns. Jot down the items in the first list on the left and the items in the second list on the right. Then discuss these in light of *vocation*, or a sense of calling (through either paid work or other life pursuit).

NOW

1. What do you notice about the list of skills on the left?
2. How about the list of passions on the right?

a. We're grateful to Chris Lopez and our teammate Roslyn Hernández for their insights on the world of superheroes and their connection to teenagers' search for answers to the 3 big questions.

GOD

3. Think for a moment about how you could take a skill or two from the first column and combine it with a passion or two from the second column to create a potential vocation. What vocations might be a good fit? (If possible, come up with three or four—or more!—vocations. They don't have to be limited to jobs or careers.)

4. What does this exercise tell you about how a community can help us discern new possibilities?

HOW

5. Which of these vocations is most appealing? What makes it appealing?

6. What other vocations that we've named today stand out to you? What about them stands out?

7. What next steps could you take to better understand how any of these vocations align with God's STORY for your life?

Conversations about STORY Elsewhere in the Bible

To help you appreciate the full meaning of God inviting us into his STORY, we encourage you and young people to explore the following Scripture passages, which are great to meditate on, memorize, send by text, or compile into a small group or youth ministry teaching series.

- Joshua 1:1–18, especially verse 7: As characters in God's STORY, we can be strong and courageous.
- Isaiah 52:1–12, especially verse 7: We have the beautiful opportunity to invite others to play their part in God's STORY.

For Families

To teenagers, an adult's questions can feel like nagging—especially when that adult is their parent, stepparent, or caregiver. We just want to know when our kid will reply to their grandma's text or follow up with their teacher about a missed math test. But in their ears, it sounds like badgering.

That's why I (Kara) am so grateful for this three-word question: *What's your plan?*[a]

In the last twenty-four hours, I've asked my teenagers the following:

What's your plan for cleaning your room?

What's your plan for today?

What's your plan for your meeting with your college counselor?

Our kids feel like they have agency (which they do!), and I get (at least some) assurance that they are on top of things.

- Jeremiah 1:4–19, especially verse 5: Before our birth, God knew us and the part of his STORY that best fits us.

- Matthew 16:21–28, especially verses 24–25: As we deny ourselves and lose our lives in devotion to God's STORY, we end up finding life.

- Romans 12:1–2, especially verse 1: As characters in God's STORY, we worshipfully offer ourselves as holy sacrifices.

- 1 Corinthians 12:12–31, especially verses 27–31: We each are given different gifts that contribute to God's STORY.

a. Credit for this zinger goes to Christine Carter, *The New Adolescence: Raising Happy and Successful Teens in an Age of Anxiety and Distraction* (Dallas: BenBella Books, 2020), 25.

- Ephesians 2:1–10, especially verse 10: We are God's handiwork, created to do good works as part of God's STORY.
- Philippians 2:1–11, especially verses 3–4: As we are invited into God's STORY, we look for opportunities to selflessly serve others.

Justice-Oriented Connections about Purpose

Purpose is better fostered than forced. Few connections nurture teenagers' grasp of being an active character in God's STORY more than seeking *justice*.

As part of discipleship, justice aims to reestablish the holistic flourishing, or *shalom*, in our relationships with God, others, nature, and ourselves.[10] Put more simply, justice is devoted to *righting wrongs*.[11]

The Hebrew word for "justice" is *mishpat*, which is used 421 times in the Old Testament, including the following:

- "Do not pervert justice; do not show partiality to the poor or favoritism to the great, but judge your neighbor fairly" (Lev. 19:15).
- "For I, the LORD, love justice" (Isa. 61:8).
- "He has shown you, O mortal, what is good. And what does the Lord require of you? To act justly and to love mercy and to walk humbly with your God" (Mic. 6:8).

As we saw in chapter 8, the churched teenagers in our study already find purpose by serving others. That's a good first step, but it's several paces short of the systemic solutions required to right wrongs and fully experience God's STORY.

Reflecting on Jesus' parable of the Good Samaritan in the midst of the turmoil of the 1960s civil rights movement and concurrent war in Vietnam, Martin Luther King Jr. urged:

> On the one hand we are called to play the Good Samaritan on life's roadside; but that will be only an initial act. One day we must come to see that the whole Jericho road must be transformed so that men and women will not be constantly beaten and robbed as they make their journey on life's highway. True compassion is more than flinging a coin to a beggar; it is not haphazard and superficial. It comes to see that an edifice which produces beggars needs restructuring.[12]

Translating Dr. King's words to you and young people today, we believe that serving food at the local homeless shelter is a purposeful act, but it is not an act of justice. Justice calls us to ask *why* people are hungry and homeless in our community and then compels us to work together to do something about it.

Justice Connections with Your Own Deep Gladness

"The place God calls you to is the place where your deep gladness and the world's deep hunger meet."[13] Implied in this memorable description of justice-seeking vocation by Frederick Buechner is that each of us—Brad and I, you, the teenagers you're closest to—has different sources of "deep gladness." We each resonate with different plotlines in God's grand adventure of righting wrongs.

Take some time with a young person to figure out, whether it's through a paying job or a purposeful hobby, the best intersection between the world's deep hunger and their own deep gladness by doing the following:

1. Pay attention to news stories about injustice in your community, country, or world.

2. Collect social media stories of people (especially teenagers) who are righting wrongs around them.

3. Invite students to name one local injustice that moves them.

4. Discuss any injustices they've personally experienced and how those encounters might spark particular passions.

5. Ask teenagers to name a few peers or adults they respect who are actively working—and making sacrifices—for the flourishing of others. Help students unpack why they admire them, and if possible invite those peers or adults to spend an hour with them so they can learn more about their work.

As students process the world's hunger and their own deep gladness, you might want to follow one church's example and encourage them to draft simple "Calling Credos." Students are presented with the following simple statement and are invited to fill in two blanks:

God put me on earth to _____ *so that* _____.

Our church's motto is "Love God, love others, make a difference." That purpose is really consistent throughout all the ministries—from our youth ministry to our outreaches. That purpose is our biggest theme and probably what I've most gained from our church. —Samuel

---

Connections to Justice as a Process, Not an Event

Today's young people are channeling their passion to serve through protests, marches, sit-ins, and fresh cries for equity and justice using social media.

But does service transform them? Of the more than two million US teenagers who experience faith-based service and mission trips every year, five out of six report that those trips don't leave a lasting mark on their lives.[14]

Based on our last decade's review of research geared to deepen the impact of justice, we urge you to think of purposeful service and activism as a three-step process.[15]

Step 1: Before. A lasting service experience starts when we help teenagers adequately *prepare* for the sometimes menial and often mind-blowing justice experiences awaiting them. That can be done through prayer, focused conversations on why they're serving or protesting, and Scripture passages they hope to keep in mind, as well as a study of the culture, needs, and resources of those with whom they're serving.

Step 2: During. Enhance the impact of justice work by helping young people *reflect* through prayerful discussions about the assets they've seen in the community, how their service or vigil is part of God's ongoing work, and what they've learned about people in the community, themself, and their faith.

Step 3: After. Deepen the impression of service by helping students *connect* the dots between the public school they painted on Sunday after church and the homeless woman they pass every Monday morning on their way to class. Make sure you schedule time immediately after serving, as well as a week or two later, for them to share how serving has connected them to God's STORY along with how they

For Leaders

In order to experience justice as a process rather than just an event, one youth ministry in Pella, Iowa, asked their student house groups spread throughout town to adopt the neighborhood they met in each Wednesday night. First, they spent time listening to God and residents, collectively discerning how they might fill a neighborhood need.

Those thoughtful efforts culminated in a one-day Love Pella Service Day. Hundreds of students and adults surged into the community and delivered meals, helped with yard work, created murals, and hosted a block party complete with inflatables and grilled hamburgers. One group even sponsored a diaper drive that netted over $6,500 in diapers for a local charity! To cap off the Love Pella Service Day, students joined together after the day was over for reflection, prayer, and sharing.

plan to continue serving and inviting others to join them. If young people have led an online or in-person protest or justice event, think with them about the next logical steps that can help flesh out God's STORY.

As you team with young people in justice work, you'll increase its impact by focusing on the *quality of reflection* rather than the *quantity of results*. According to one researcher on purpose, "Rather than participating in activity after activity, youth should be encouraged to participate in fewer activities and to reflect more on the meaning derived from each one."[16]

Our Stories as Adults Expand Too

Determined to launch justice conversations and connections with teenagers, Jen, a youth pastor outside Chicago, planned to draft a new "purpose" curriculum for her church's youth ministry. Needing help, Jen sought out Linda, a retired religion and ethics teacher who still had great passion for teenagers.

As soon as Jen asked if Linda would like to help, Linda burst into tears. Linda had battled cancer and had been in remission for two years. But unbeknownst to Jen, the cancer had recurred. Linda was still absorbing the news and had shared it with only her closest friends and family.

As she clutched tissues, Linda explained, "When you have a recurrence of cancer, people ask what's on your bucket list. For most people, it's travel. For me, it's ministry to teenagers. I've been praying for a way to serve from my house during my chemotherapy. Jen, you are giving me that chance."

So every week for the following months, Jen sent Linda the discussions and activities she had drafted. Linda ripped them apart, adding depth, relevance, and clearer connections to God's STORY. Jen reflected following Linda's death, "Linda was the most creative person I've ever encountered. I kept thanking her every week for all she added, and she kept thanking me for letting her use her gifts in a way that was literally life-giving for her."

When you and I help young people grow in purpose through God's STORY, our own stories get bigger and better also.

Christ-Centered Purpose Recap

In this chapter, we provide a handful of summary phrases for you and your teenagers. We've geared these statements to serve not just as a recap but also as reminders of conversations and connections. Once you have chosen a purpose message you want to remember, the next step is to create a system that reminds you of that truth every day.

You and your young people might want to *set a daily alarm on your phones*—to go off perhaps in the morning as you're getting ready or in the evening as you're winding down—to remind you to think about one or more of these divine truths.

Or maybe go "low tech" and *write God's better message on an index card* you display on your bathroom mirror, car dashboard, or office bookshelf.

Perhaps you and your students can *take turns texting important messages* to each other, strengthening your mutual commitment to live into God's greater STORY.

Whatever you choose, make sure *you* also do whatever you ask of your young people so that you too can share your progress in realizing your true purpose.

Here is a list of messages you can draw from:

- We're invited into God's greater STORY.
- God's STORY is a bigger and better story.
- "I cannot answer the question, 'What ought I to do?' unless I first answer the question, 'Of which story am I a part?'"[17]
- God's story has six acts, and I'm helping to live out the fifth.
- Good. Guilt. Grace. God's people. Gratitude.
- "God is the larger context and plot in which our stories find themselves."[18]
- I'm finding my superpower.
- From performance to purpose.
- Justice means righting wrongs.
- "The place God calls you to is the place where your deep gladness and the world's deep hunger meet."[19]

REFLECT and APPLY

1. Which of the conversation or justice connections in this chapter would be best for you and the young people you know?

2. What difference might that conversation or connection make in you and in your young people's sense of purpose?

3. What might you and your young people have to adjust in your relationships or routines to make time for that change? What would make it worthwhile to make that change?

4. What prayer would you like to offer as you help young people, as well as yourself, understand that we're all invited into God's greater STORY?

PART V

QUESTIONS
DISRUPTED

CURRENT CHRIST-CENTERED

Discipleship
Journey

Conversations and Connections in Tough Times

I feel like the chapters of my life would be centered around my emotional state, because I have my highs and lows and they really differ throughout the year.

Karie

When we set out to write this book in 2020, we had no way of predicting what would unfold. On Friday, March 13, my (Brad's) kids went to school like normal. The local school board had decided the night before to keep school in session and watch the progress of the coronavirus, which just recently had been labeled a "pandemic." But by midday, the district had changed course. Students left school that Friday without really saying goodbye to anyone, thinking they'd be back after an extra week of spring break.

That extra week turned into an extra two months. School never resumed that spring—or for much of the next year. Children, teenagers, and young adults nationwide entered a months-long quarantine at home, separated from friends, teachers, and coaches. For some, this meant monotony and stir-crazy angst. For others whose parents lost jobs, whose family members worked on the front lines of the pandemic, or whose homes weren't emotionally or physically safe, it meant daily fear of the worst. And for far too many, the worst did come. Death visited their homes, extended family, or friends.

We all have our personal stories of the effects of the COVID-19 pandemic. My oldest daughter, Anna, lost many of the most-anticipated moments of senior year. Prom. Grad night. Graduation itself. There were a few school friends and favorite teachers she may never see in person again. This major life celebration dissolved into one loss after another, followed by the loss of an on-campus first fall semester of college. On top of that, her grandfather (my father) died, and we were unable to travel to Kentucky to attend the funeral or hug our family. It was all so surreal.

Similarly, Kara's youngest, Jessica, lost many of the most-anticipated parts of eighth grade, thanks to COVID-19's abrupt end of a fourteen-year streak for the Powells at the same K–8 school. The teachers and administrators valiantly rallied for a Socially Distant Parking Lot Eighth Grade Graduation (drive-in movie style), but it was a far cry from what Jessica had seen her older brother and sister experience in years prior.

And there was more. While the pandemic raged on, bringing with it a stark economic downturn, something else emerged. Incidences of racial violence leapt to the forefront of public consciousness. The violence wasn't new, but in a series of dramatic moments, long-standing wounds were ripped open by the sequential deaths of Ahmaud Arbery, Breonna Taylor, and George Floyd. An undercurrent of injustice was elevated to a national crisis. Some peaceful protests turned into riots. Young people (including those in my and Kara's families) raised their voices alongside those of adults, often leading the way in organizing gatherings for weeks following. Across the country, crowds gathered to speak up for the human dignity of Black lives.

To young people already wrestling with the 3 big questions of identity, belonging, and purpose, the world felt on fire. Disruption ruled the day.

The Power of Disruption

Disruptive became one of the most commonly used descriptors in 2020. Plans were crushed. Dreams were deferred, or altogether decimated. Anger spurred action around racial injustice.

In the midst of so much upheaval, surprises broke through. Many teenagers got creative during quarantine. They made music, baked bread, encouraged one another from a distance, and found ways to help their communities.

They also organized to call for change. During just one week in Nashville, six teenagers orchestrated a march via Twitter that drew over ten thousand peaceful protesters. These young women—all ages fourteen to sixteen—founded Teens for Equality together, despite never having met in person until the march. Reflecting on the impact of the five-hour protest, co-organizer Kennedy Green shared, "I do believe in the future because there are a lot of kids who are changing the future, trying to end white supremacy and hatred and racism in America."[1]

Kennedy, we believe with you.

Indeed, laws and policies started changing. Monuments started coming down. A deeper commitment grew to understand and honor the Black experience. It wasn't the end of the road by any measure, but it felt like rounding a new corner.

Disruption, it turns out, can be a powerful catalyst for change.

Stability and Instability

Life is full of instabilities and interruptions. Most of the time we do not anticipate them or welcome them. Our parents divorce. We move to another state. Our stepmom loses her job. A brother becomes chronically ill. We survive a traumatic car accident.

Even instabilities like not getting the position they hoped to play on a team can throw a student off. Or failing a test in their best subject. Or (circling back to Kara's story in our opening chapter) losing a school election.

But here's a reframe: instability can be a greenhouse for growth in identity, belonging, and purpose. Disruptions till the soil—or transplant us into altogether different gardens—in

Being flung into many different locations and environments helped me learn to adapt. Because I have experienced so many different settings, it helps me understand who I am and how I can belong. –Arthur

Despite looking on the positive side of adversity in this chapter, we feel compelled to acknowledge that there are plenty of disruptions from which we want to shield young people altogether. Experiences of abuse, poverty, or racial discrimination come quickly to mind. No one should have to live through the pain and dehumanization of any of these often-traumatic stressors; it is unthinkable that we allow and even support systems that propagate all three—frequently for the same young people. Naming the power of adversity for growth in no way means these atrocities are positive or justified.[a]

which young people learn to put down new roots, sprout new branches, and eventually produce a harvest.[2]

We naturally look for that growth in the positive disruptions. When my (Kara's) son Nathan went to college, we anticipated it would stretch him in all kinds of new ways. And sure enough, the first time he returned home on break, he felt different. His identity and purpose in particular grew so much during freshman year. While he's still close to Dave and me, Nathan is clearer about where he's similar to and different from us. He's more *adult*.

Whether we experience disruptions as positive or negative, we don't get to escape them; we have to find our way through. We have to make meaning from our hardships. As leaders and parents, we may want to protect kids from all kinds of struggles, but we can't. And even if we could, we would be hindering them from the growth they need.[3]

We've been giving you tips throughout this book for better conversations and connections around the 3 big questions.

a. Research abounds on the impact of Adverse Childhood Experiences, or ACEs. They consist of traumatic events that occur in childhood or adolescence (from birth to age seventeen). According to the CDC, ACEs "are linked to chronic health problems, mental illness, and substance misuse in adulthood. ACEs can also negatively impact education and job opportunities." "Preventing Adverse Childhood Experiences," Centers for Disease Control and Prevention, accessed June 22, 2020, https://www.cdc.gov/violenceprevention/childabuseand neglect/aces/fastfact.html.

Here are a few more to help you walk with young people through their toughest days.

Conversations about Tough Times

If you've worked with young people very long, you know that painful experiences can open doors to some of the best conversations—often along the themes of identity, belonging, and purpose. When life is hard, we can be present to teenagers and help them say an everyday "Yes" to Jesus, even or maybe especially during hardship.

A Conversation to Process Painful Experiences

When a young person first talks about a disruption or loss, they may be very emotional or just the opposite—emotionally flat. Either way, start by trying to understand what happened from their perspective and how it is impacting them. The teenager's perception of what happened is more important than sorting out facts and details. Be careful not to push too hard soon after a troubling event; sometimes a young person needs time before they are ready to process very much.

NOW

1. Tell me what happened. (Give them time to share in their own words, even if you already know the story.)
2. What were you feeling?
3. What are you feeling now?
4. What do you think you need right now?

GOD

5. Where is God in the midst of this? (Does it seem like God is active? Silent? Unavailable? Not listening? Very present with you?)

6. What do you think God thinks or feels about this situation?

7. What can you do to remember God is with you right now?

HOW

Instead of diving too quickly into problem solving, you might start by asking the following:

8. What kind of help do you want? I can keep listening and help you think about some next steps, or we can pause for now and pick this up another time.

9. Who else can you talk to about this?

10. What is one next step you can take? What kind of support do you need to take it?

11. How can I pray for you?

A Conversation for When a Teenager Experiences Violence in Their Community

Growing up in the span from Sandy Hook to Parkland, this generation is well aware that no community is immune to violence. In the wake of a local traumatic event like a neighborhood or school shooting, here are some conversation tools to use with a young person.

NOW

Use phrases that help them feel safe to share. Start with basic questions.

1. What do you know about what happened? What did you experience?

   Assess what they've heard, seen, or processed already. This will give you a baseline for what else to ask or say. Try to match your response with their level of awareness. The following open-ended phrases might prompt young people to speak more freely, especially when they're confused, sad, or scared.

2. Tell me more . . . (about what you're feeling; what you mean; what you're experiencing).

3. I wonder how . . . (that person might feel; we can help; this is impacting you).

4. Let me know if . . . (you want to talk more later; you have a friend who's struggling with this; you start to feel anxious or afraid).

GOD

5. How have you sensed God through this experience? Does it feel more like God is present or absent?

6. What questions are you wrestling with?

HOW

Chances are good that the young people in your life will pose questions for which you don't have answers. Here's a useful four-word response to keep handy: "I don't know, but . . ."[4] There are a number of ways to use this simple phrase to create a safe space with a teenager:

7. I don't know, but . . . (that's an important question; I wonder that too; how about if we meet again to talk about it?).

As in any conversation with a teenager in pain, be mindful of moving too quickly to problem solving. In the wake of tragedy, lead with questions such as these:

8. What feels helpful right now?
9. Is there anything you need? (Have you eaten? How are you sleeping?)
10. Who else is helping you through this?
11. When would it be helpful to check in again?

Be attentive for signs of post-traumatic stress, which include feeling hopeless, numb, on guard, or scared; increased mood swings; having trouble sleeping or eating; acting out; or other physical distress. If the young person is experiencing these symptoms, start by encouraging them to take a break from news related to the events for a while. If signs of post-traumatic stress linger more than a couple of weeks, it's a good idea to help the young person find professional help.

Dr. Cynthia Eriksson, a trauma specialist in Fuller's School of Psychology and Marriage and Family Therapy, offers these suggestions as we journey with young people experiencing post-traumatic stress:

> We need to let them express whatever is going on in their minds in terms of their relationship with God. Our pastoral and parental tendency is to come in with some sort of answer to help them not doubt anymore. However, the most important first step is to be heard, even if what needs to be said are horrible thoughts toward God. Let go of the need to be a theological educator and stay in the moment in a pastoral place with the young person. Acknowledge that it's often hard to see God in the midst of these experiences.
>
> If we turn to someone in the midst of doubt and say, "God is going to get you through this," we risk the possibility of the person feeling guilty or judged for not being able to hold on to that hope themselves. I'll never forget when I discovered

Psalm 88. It doesn't end with professions of God's faithfulness, but rather something like, "I'm going to die." There are moments in life where we do not see the hopeful side, and it seems impossible to hold on to God's goodness. For many, it might take a long time to see God in the midst of what happened. The most caring thing is to hear the doubts and not try to "fix" the person or convince him or her otherwise.[5]

When a Friend Attempts or Dies by Suicide

Tragically, most young people will know a teenager who attempts or dies by suicide, whether a friend or a local peer. When suicide hits close to home, adults often feel helpless and even paralyzed about what to do next.

Law enforcement chaplain and Fuller faculty member Mary Glenn has been a first responder in a number of these situations. She shares the following guidelines for anyone walking with young people through this particular season of grief.[a]

1. *Offer the ministry of presence.* Grief needs community, not isolation. We can embody the peace and presence of God by simply being with others, sitting in the midst of their pain. Sometimes we may not say much of anything at all.
2. *Avoid clichés and quick-fix answers,* such as "Everything will be okay," which can just bring more pain. When someone ends their life, it changes those around them—things won't ever be "the same." But we can share that eventually we will move forward after loss.
3. *Face down the guilt, shame, and anger.* We may feel like we should have known and could have done something. Going down that road won't bring them back. We cannot change what happened. But the emotions we feel are real, and we need to create healthy space for feelings to be expressed.
4. *Acknowledge the impact of the death imprint.* When we see or experience something traumatic, our brains take a picture

of what we see or can imagine. That death imprint stays with us. Smells, sights, and sounds might stir up painful memories. Be patient and sensitive with young people when this happens—often unexpectedly.

5. *Reinforce that God is with us.* In the midst of tragic loss and pain, we can remind one another that God is with us. Jesus identifies with the depths of our suffering and trauma as one who came near and took them on himself. We can cling to the hope that somehow God will make a way forward through loss.

6. *Refer as needed.* Professional therapy, grief counseling, or pastoral counseling may be a helpful next step. Be prepared with referrals to local helpers for young people and families. You may also want to point them to the National Suicide Prevention Lifeline (1-800-273-TALK or suicidepreventionlifeline.org) or, particularly for students of color, the Steve Fund Crisis Text Line (text STEVE to 741-741 or visit stevefund.org/crisistextline).

Here are a few practical phrases you can use to avoid minimizing pain or promising that everything will be okay:

- "I am so sorry that you are going through this. I am here with you now; you are not alone."
- "Together we will find you the help you need."
- "I may not know exactly what you are feeling, but I care about you and I want to help."

Connections about Tough Times through Lament

"Why are you so far off? Why have you hidden your face from me?"

When bad things happen, it's common to question, be angry with, and struggle to trust God. The most appropriate response to these kinds of reactions is to lament. Lament is a God-given tool to help us pray and worship our way

a. Mary Glenn, "In the Aftermath of Suicide: Helping Communities Heal," Fuller Youth Institute, February 26, 2014, https://fulleryouthinstitute.org/articles/in-the-aftermath-of-suicide. Thanks to Aaron Rosales and Hannah Lee for additional insights on this section.

through pain and tragedy.[6] While uncomfortable and sometimes awkward to read, the psalms of lament (there are over sixty-five of them) in the Bible give us language for crying out to God in ways we might not normally find acceptable. Perhaps that's exactly why they exist.

As youth workers or parents, we may fear taking students to places of honest doubt, anger, and disappointment with God. However, failing to create an environment for authentic lament can result in spiritually and psychologically short-circuiting the necessary healing process. Through the practice of lament, we have the opportunity to offer the hope of Christ and his reorienting power to lives that have been plunged into disorientation.[7]

A Connection through Reading and Praying Psalms of Lament

Whether one-on-one or in a small group context, read psalms of lament together. Consider for starters Psalms 6, 10, 13, 42, 61, 74, 77, 80, 88, 126, and 142.

If these psalms are new to your young people, you might start with Psalm 13. In just six verses, Psalm 13 models the rhythm of lament—from honest despair to petition to hope. It begins with "How long, LORD? Will you forget me forever?" (v. 1) and moves to "but I trust in your unfailing love" (v. 5). In the middle is a passionate request for God to "look on me and answer . . . or I will sleep in death" (v. 3).

Do one or more of the following as a next step to help young people interact with psalms of lament:

- Ask reflection questions such as "Is it okay to say these kinds of things to God?" and "What surprises you about this psalm?"

- Read the psalm several times, inviting students to journal their own prayer for a few minutes.
- Pray the words of the psalm as a start to students' own prayers of lament, encouraging them to add verses of their own after you finish the psalm itself.
- Have students write an original lament based on this pattern:
  - How long, Lord?
  - Help! Answer me!
  - Yet I will trust you . . .
- Ask students to draw, paint, or sculpt a response, visually expressing their own losses.
- Light candles, representing their laments.
- Ask students to pray the psalm every day for a week and come back together to share reflections on this practice.

Be sure to debrief these practices, talking through their feelings of comfort or discomfort in approaching God in these ways.

Lament Connections through Music

Since the psalms in the Bible were originally sung, we know music has been used to share raw feelings with God for thousands of years, maybe since the beginning of time. Music is deeply linked with emotional expression—especially for teenagers. Reassure students that the feelings they let out when listening to their favorite songs are ones they can bring to God too.

Either one-on-one or in a group context, invite students to think about their favorite sad song—maybe it's a breakup song, maybe it expresses anger or loss. Encourage them to name all the emotions they feel when they listen to the song.

Be prepared to listen without judgment, even if young people share songs that include explicit lyrics or that you think hold little value (musical or otherwise). This is a time to listen and affirm![8]

Musically inclined teenagers can be encouraged to create their own songs inspired by lament. Let them know it's okay if they want to keep this kind of song to themselves but that you can also be a safe person to share their music with even if they aren't comfortable sharing it broadly.

You may want to have a song of your own ready to play as an example and share why it helps you express grief, hurt, or heartache. You might have a story about why this song has voiced your lament in a particularly difficult time or has reminded you of the goodness of God. You can also search online for "psalm lament songs" to find one or more recorded songs that might help your young people share their sadness, fears, and confusion with God. (Do this ahead of time. There's also plenty of funky stuff online using these search terms.)

Lament Connections Elsewhere in the Bible

Since we have already highlighted laments in the book of Psalms, here we look to other helpful texts that can be compelling to meditate on, memorize, send by text, or compile into a small group or youth ministry teaching series.

- Genesis 16:1–15, especially verse 13: The story of Abram and Hagar elevates an unseen and enslaved girl as one who was seen by God (and who in the Old Testament is the first to give God a name—"the God who sees me").

- Job (the entire book is filled with lament!), especially Job 23:1–12: We may not see God, but God has not left us alone.
- Isaiah 40:25–31, especially verse 31: God gives strength to the weary and to those who hope in the Lord.
- Lamentations 3:1–33, especially verses 22–23: Despite incredible loss, God's faithfulness never ends, and his mercy is new every morning.
- John 11:1–44, especially verses 21–35: When Jesus' friend Lazarus died, he was confronted with the grief of Lazarus's sisters and he wept. Jesus offers himself as "the resurrection and the life" (v. 25), the ultimate hope in the face of human death.

Saying "Yes" to Jesus in Our Struggles

In the midst of walking through hard moments in young people's lives, we can help them keep saying an everyday "Yes" to Jesus. As we do, our hope is not to produce happiness, success, wealth, or even stability on the other side of instability.

Our hope is to help young people *flourish*.

We believe all people are created to flourish. This is God's ultimate hope for humanity. And we believe the identity, belonging, and purpose journeys of young people direct them toward flourishing, even when the road is paved with adversity. That's where our discipleship is heading: our everyday "Yes" to Jesus is always another step toward participating in the inbreaking good news of God for the life of the world.

Grace-Filled Realism

If you're feeling overwhelmed at the prospects of walking with teenagers through their most painful experiences, remember that you don't need to be perfect in your caregiving. Accompaniment itself is often a healing gift.

Pastoral care scholar Edward Wimberly writes about the pressure we put on ourselves when we care for others. He asserts that we can offer a "good enough empathy" in place of trying to achieve some impossibly perfect standard. We can help young people with "grace-filled realism," which "enables us to make significant—but not unflawed—contributions to the lives of others. It is not driven by fear of falling short of an impossible external standard, or law, or expectation. Rather, grace-filled realism is caregiving nurtured by a transcendent love that motivates and energizes."[a]

The young people in your life need more than a thin gospel;[9] they need a robust vision of the good news of Jesus that holds up under their greatest trials. Your accompaniment on their discipleship journey can both point to and model what it looks like to say "Yes" to Jesus even when life is hard.

Keep Paying Attention

Kara and I (Brad), and our entire interview team, were changed by spending so many hours listening to the teenagers you've met in these pages. We didn't always hear what we expected.

They challenged our assumptions.

They gave language and stories to statistics.

a. Edward P. Wimberly, *Recalling Our Own Stories: Spiritual Renewal for Religious Caregivers* (Minneapolis: Fortress, 2019), 11.

Our interview teammate Jennifer Guerra Aldana reflected on the process: "I walked in wondering who would want to talk about these things with a total stranger, and walked out thinking, *Who* wouldn't *want to?* So I sat with the interview protocols one night and started journaling through them. I ended up in tears. These reflections showed up in my therapy sessions, and I thought, '*Everybody should be doing this for themselves first!*'"

I (Brad) have often thought back to my interviews with Armando. A recent high school graduate who lives with his grandmother, Armando is figuring out what it means to be a young adult while remaining tethered to his family. I'll never forget his description of his relationship with his grandmother. He really loves her, but "a little space to breathe would be perfect for me." As a parent of a daughter also trying to become an adult, that expression hit home for me.

I was moved by Armando's resilience. He was born in Mexico and moved to the US at age three. He's never known his father. Because of some complicated family dynamics and his mom's immigration status, Armando didn't see her for eight years—his entire adolescence. Despite these hardships, Armando is really motivated by helping others. He wants to be seen as a hero someday. When we met, he was planning a career in firefighting and wanted to become the first in his family to graduate from college. He reflected, "I feel like I belong now—how do I say this—*in this world*. I feel like now I have a purpose."

And I was inspired by Armando's deep faith. He described God to me as "someone you love, who you have faith in, regardless if you can see him or not. God is that person who will always be there for you. God is our friend, our father—our best friend actually. Once you start talking to him you feel his presence and know he's there, you know he's listening to you. God is that person you can't live without."

Given all Armando has lived through, his is a remarkably mature picture of God.

As you spend time with the teenagers in your life, keep paying attention. Keep listening. Become a student of the young people around you. They have so much to teach all of us about how they're wrestling with the 3 big questions.

The questions will certainly change them—but the journey will also change you.

Big Question	Focus	Description	Current Answers	Christ-Centered Answer
Who am I?	Identity	Our view of ourselves	*I am...* • what others expect. • not _____ enough. • my image. • more than my label.	I'm ENOUGH because of Jesus.
Where do I fit?	Belonging	Our connection with others	*I fit...* • where I feel safe to be me. • where we share _____. • where I feel like I'm needed.	I belong WITH God's people.
What difference can I make?	Purpose	Our contribution to the world	*I make a difference...* • when I'm helping others. • when I follow the script. • when I get to make choices about my life. • when I'm headed toward a good future.	I'm invited into God's greater STORY.

REFLECT and APPLY

1. Which of the conversation or lament connection ideas in this chapter would be best for you and the young people you know?

2. Looking back over the book as a whole, what are the one to three insights that stand out to you most as you think about your relationships with teenagers?

3. Identify one next step you'd like to take to act on an idea from this book. Write a note to yourself or set a calendar reminder to get started this week!

Our Interview Participants

Name (alias)	Gender	Race-Ethnicity[1]	Region	Grade	Community	SES[2]
Armando	M	Latino	West Coast	Post-HS	Urban	Lower
Arthur	M	Asian American	West Coast	12	Urban	Middle
Ben	M	White	Midwest	9	Suburban	Middle
Claudia	F	Latina	West Coast	12	Urban	Unsure
Daniel	M	African American/ Asian American	West Coast	11	Urban	Lower
Gabriel	M	Latino	West Coast	12	Urban	Lower
Hailey	F	White	West Coast	12	Suburban	Lower
Hannah	F	Latina/Asian American	West Coast	Post-HS	Suburban	Middle
Isabel	F	Asian American	West Coast	Post-HS	Suburban	Middle
Janelle	F	African American	West Coast	11	Urban	Lower
Jason	M	African American	East Coast	10	Suburban	Middle
Jerome	M	African American	West Coast	12	Urban	Unsure

Name (alias)	Gender	Race-Ethnicity[1]	Region	Grade	Community	SES[2]
Karie	F	Asian American	West Coast	9	Suburban	Middle
Kevin	M	African American/ Asian American	West Coast	12	Suburban	Upper middle
Leo	M	Arab American	West Coast	11	Suburban	Lower
Lilly	F	Asian American	West Coast	12	Urban	Unsure
Michael	M	White	Midwest	12	Rural	Upper middle
Natalie	F	African American/ White	South	10	Suburban	Middle
Nick	M	White	South	11	Suburban	Upper middle
Rebekah	F	White	South	12	Suburban	Upper middle
Samuel	M	Asian American	West Coast	12	Suburban	Middle
Sebastian	M	Latino	West Coast	11	Urban	Lower
Simone	F	African American	East Coast	10	Suburban	Upper middle
Sofia	F	Latina	West Coast	12	Urban	Unsure
Steve	M	White	South	12	Rural	Lower
Sue	F	Asian American	South	11	Suburban	Middle
Taylor	Non-binary	White	West Coast	11	Suburban	Upper middle

Over 170 Questions to Ask a Teenager

To help you have better conversations and connections with the young people important to you, we wanted you to have access to our full list of interview questions.[1] We scheduled three separate two-hour interviews with each student and followed a research protocol that included securing parental consent (for minors) and participant consent for the interviews to be recorded and for de-identified data to be used for this project. We've removed interviewee instructions, verbal consent, reminders, and transitions between sections, leaving just the basic questions for you.

Interview 1

Warm-Up Questions

1. Tell me a little bit about a typical day in your life. What do you do, where do you go, who are you around, that kind of thing?

2. I see from your survey that you're a (year in school) at (name of school). What's that's like?

3. Outside of school, do you have particular interests, sports, or things you like to do when you can?

4. What kinds of social media platforms, games, or apps do you use a lot these days?

Life Chapters

5. Sometimes people might think about their life like a book that has different chapters. If you were going to write about your life or someone wrote a book about your life so far, how would you break it up into chapters? You don't have to give me all the details of those chapters, but pretend I'm thumbing through that book and getting a sense for your life so far. Tell me about those chapters.

   If the participant struggles with this question or asks for clarity, you might say something like, "There's no right or wrong way to answer. One person might talk about their life based on different stages like preschool, elementary school, that kind of thing. Another might identify events that mark big changes in their life, like a family move or the birth of a little brother."

6. Is there a particular chapter that stands out the most to you, maybe because it was important in some way? Tell me a little more about that time in your life.

Overview of Religious Life

7. About how long have you been part of your church?

8. What's the church like? What kinds of things do you do as part of the church?

   Follow up as appropriate to get a sense of frequency of participation. For example, "About how often do you go to worship/sing/volunteer/etc.?"

9. Could you tell me about your youth group or whatever your church does with young people your age?

10. Who else from your family participates in church, and how involved are they?

11. Do your parents attend this church?

12. Do either of your parents attend church elsewhere?

13. And just to clarify, are your parents married?

14. Thinking back again across your life so far, tell me more about your experience of church and faith. Would you say you "grew up" in church? What has that been like for you?

15. Can you think of any particularly important moments in your faith that stand out to you?

16. Sometimes when people think about their experiences of being part of a church, there are stories that come to mind—they might be of positive or negative experiences, or just something that kind of reminds them of church. Is there a story like that that comes to mind for you when you think about church?

17. Sometimes people have spiritual experiences or somehow encounter God in ways that aren't necessarily

connected to being part of a church. Is there an experience like that that comes to mind for you?

This question is intentionally broad, but if this is confusing to the participant, you might rephrase as "Are there ways you encounter God outside of church?"

18. Do one or two people come to mind who have impacted your faith? Tell me a little bit about them and why they've been important to you.

19. How would you describe God to a friend?

    If the participant struggles, reword as "Often we form ideas or images about God based on our experience of church or what we've been taught about God by our church or family. Do you have a particular image or description you associate with God?"

Identity

20. When you ask yourself, "Who am I?" what sorts of words or phrases come to mind?

21. How would your friends describe you? If I asked one of your friends to tell me "Who is _____?" what do you think they would say?

22. What about your family—what would they say about you?

23. Would you say your clothes represent who you are? How so?

24. What do you think other people might miss or get wrong about you?

25. Think about a time when you really felt like you knew who you were. Could you tell me about that experience?

26. Can you think of a time when you *didn't* feel like you knew who you were? What happened that caused you to feel that way?

27. How often do you think about who you are as a person? Is it something that comes to mind a lot, sometimes, or not much at all?

Belonging

28. Now let's talk about your experiences of belonging. If you were to ask yourself, "Where do I belong?" what comes to mind?

29. Think about a time when you really felt included. Can you describe an experience like that or share a story? What was it like?

30. What about a time you felt left out or excluded? What caused those feelings?

31. How often do you think about whether you belong somewhere or with a particular group? Is it something that comes to mind a lot, sometimes, or not much at all?

32. Where do you really feel like you belong, no matter what?

    If the interviewee says nowhere, follow up with "I wonder why you don't feel like there's anywhere you belong no matter what?" If they give a positive response, ask, "Tell me more about that (place, group, family). What about it/them makes you feel like you always belong?"

Purpose

33. Now I'm going to ask some questions about purpose, which some people think about as a sense of how our lives and what we do matter in the world. Would you say you think about those kinds of things a lot, sometimes, or not much at all?

34. Think about a time when you were doing something and felt like it was what you were really meant to do. Maybe something you're particularly good at or really interested in or are passionate about. What were you doing? What was that experience like?

35. Can you think of a time when you didn't feel like you had much of a sense of purpose? What was that like?

36. When someone asks you, "What do you want to do with your life?" or "What do you want to be when you grow up?" what kinds of reactions do you have? What do you feel or think about?

37. Do you ever feel worried or nervous about the future? What are you anxious or nervous about when it comes to your future?

Instructions for Taking Photos

Think about the places or objects that represent somewhere or something that makes you feel as though you belong. This might be your kitchen table, a favorite park or forest, your back porch, your church, your desk or chair, almost anywhere you hang out or spend time.

For each place or object, please take one or two pictures. We are not looking for professional quality—just a snapshot that will capture the sense of the place or object. Please do try to take pictures of at least five or six places or objects, and we'll talk about them next time.

Concluding Questions

38. What was it like to share about your life like this? Was anything surprising, difficult, or helpful to talk about?

39. What else, if anything, do you want us to know about that we may be missing or may not have asked?

Interview 2

Warm-Up Question

1. Is there anything we talked about before that you want to follow up on or ask about before I get started with today's questions?

Life Stages

Last time we talked about your life like chapters in a book. (Briefly review chapters as defined by participant in previous interview.) You may have had further thoughts since the last time we met, and I'd like to ask some more specific questions about different times in your life.

Family Background

2. Let's start with some questions about your family's story. How would you describe your family's cultural background, and if your family came to the US from another country at some point, how does your family talk about that story?

3. How do you talk about your race in your family?

4. How would you describe your family's religious or faith background?

5. What are some big challenges or life changes that impacted your family before you were born? Can you tell me a story or two that are told in your family about those events?

Childhood

6. What was it like growing up in your family?

7. Who mostly took care of you as a child? What was your relationship with them like?

8. Can you think of a word to describe your parent(s)/caregiver? Does a story come to mind related to that word?

9. Tell me about your siblings. What have your relationships been like?

10. Did you or your family experience any big changes or challenges during your childhood? Can you tell me about them?

Early Adolescence (Middle School Years)

11. What was middle school like for you?

12. What were your friendships like?

13. How did you experience acceptance or rejection in middle school? Does a story come to mind?

14. What were your family relationships like during middle school?

15. Can you think of a specific example or memory that captures how you generally felt about your family during those years?

16. What ideas did you have about what you wanted to do or be when you grew up?

Late Adolescence (High School Years)
FRIENDS

17. Tell me what your friendships have been like in high school. Who are a few of your close friends, and what are they like?

18. What do you share in common, and how are you different from one another?

19. Which friends do you talk about faith with, and when you do, what do you talk about?

20. What do your friends do—or not do—that makes you feel like you really belong when you're with them?

21. If someone made a movie about you and your friends, can you think of a memorable scene that would be part of that movie? Something that kind of says it all about your friendship? Describe it to me—who is part of it? Where are you? What happens?

SCHOOL

22. Can you tell me a little bit about where you go to school?

23. How large or small is it?

24. What do you like best and least about your school?

25. What is your experience of race or culture like at school? Is there a story you can share about that?

26. Have you always gotten the grades you, or your parents, expected? What's it like when you meet your

parents' expectations for grades? What's it like when you don't?

27. How was (or how will) the decision (be) reached about either going to college and selecting which school to attend or pursuing other pathways?
28. Why was (or why will) this decision (be) made in this way?

Life beyond School

29. What kinds of things do you do outside of school besides work (sports, volunteer work, arts, etc.)?
30. What is a typical day like (game, volunteer session, etc.)?
31. How do you think these activities might or might not be connected to a sense of identity, belonging, or purpose?
32. What TV, YouTube, or other online shows do you watch most regularly?
33. Can you pick your favorite character on a show or a video personality and tell me about them?
34. In what ways do you use digital devices and social media these days? Tell me about the devices and platforms you spend time on regularly.
35. How much time do you typically spend on these devices and platforms each day? Can you tell me generally how you use that time?
36. How do you think social media affects your friendships?
37. What is it like to communicate with your friends using social media?

38. Tell me a little about the people you interact with on social media, or organizations or brands you follow. Is there a particular person or organization you really admire? Why?

39. Are there certain parts of your identity that you highlight online or choose to show online? Are there certain parts of your identity that you won't show online?

40. Do you currently hold a job outside the home? If so, what can you tell me about it?

41. Can you recall a time when you found your job especially satisfying?

42. How about especially frustrating?

43. Most everyone feels stressed or anxious sometimes. How often do you feel stressed out these days?

44. What do you think causes you the most stress or worry?

45. Circling back to your family now: Did you or your family experience any dramatic changes or challenges during high school? Can you tell me about them?

46. How has your relationship to your parents changed since you were younger?

Discussion of Photos

47. What is the story behind this picture? Tell me about where you were or what the object is.

48. Why is this place or object important to you?

49. How does this place or object make you feel you belong or remind you of something that makes you feel you belong?

50. Were there places or objects you thought about pho-
tographing but didn't, either because they aren't
nearby or for some other reason? Tell me about those
places or objects.

   If you'd like to take any more photos between now
and next time, we can look at those together then.
For this round, you can either take more belonging
photos or take some pictures that share something
about your identity or sense of purpose.

Religious Involvement, Faith, and Spirituality

51. Think about a typical time you attended church.
What is most memorable about being there?

52. Would you say that you feel a strong sense of belonging in that congregation?

53. How close do you feel to the pastor or another main
leader in your congregation?

54. How would you describe your sense of belonging
in the youth ministry or around other peers close to
your age?

55. If you were the leader of this church, what would you
change about it?

56. Are there things about your church you disagree with
or even that make you upset? Tell me about some of
those things.

57. How has faith or spirituality been talked about and
lived out in your family? Can you think of a story
that might describe that experience?

58. What does it mean, to you, to be a Christian?

59. Do you consider yourself to be a Christian? Why or why not?

60. How does being a Christian impact how you think about who you are?

61. How does being a Christian impact what you do, or your choices from day to day? Is there a story that comes to mind that might illustrate that impact?

62. How much, if at all, do you openly express your religious beliefs at school?

63. Have you ever told other kids at school about your faith or encouraged them to join your faith or to come to church with you? What was that like?

64. How often do you typically pray?

65. What are your prayers like? What are some different ways you pray?

66. What are some ways your family prays, either together or separately?

67. Have you ever experienced something that you would describe as a healing or spiritual transformation? If so, tell me more about that.

68. What are some ways the Bible has been part of your religious and spiritual life?

69. How often do you read the Bible on your own? What is that like?

70. What kinds of reactions do you have to the Bible? What kinds of feelings or questions does it raise for you?

71. Last time we talked about your sense of what God is like. Does anything else come to mind for you about who God is or what God is like?

72. Is there a story about God that sort of says it all for you?

73. Have you thought of any other experiences you've had with God or any other spiritual encounters that have been meaningful?

74. How have these experiences impacted how you think about who you are?

Interview 3

Identity

The first time we spoke you named these words or phrases as responses to the question "Who am I?": (insert words or phrases).

1. I wonder how you feel about those responses now. What do you like about these descriptions? How would you change or add to them?

2. How do you think your answers have changed over time in your life so far?

3. Have you ever felt like you had to act a certain way because a friend wanted you to? Can you tell me more about that?

4. Similarly, can you think of some ways your parents' expectations have shaped your sense of who you are? How has their picture of you, or who they want you to be, influenced your view of yourself?

5. What about expectations of people at church? Have you ever felt like you needed to be a certain way because of what people at church expected? Does a story come to mind about that?

6. How would you say your faith has impacted your sense of identity?

7. When do you tend to feel the best about yourself?

8. When do you tend to feel the worst about yourself?

9. Sometimes young people feel pressure to keep high standards or even be perfect in everything they do. Do you ever experience that pressure? What's it like for you?

Other Aspects of Identity

Gender, culture, ethnicity, and race are often talked about as important to our sense of identity. The following questions ask about these topics. For many, discussions of race or gender identity can be difficult. To narrow this down a little, just think about race and ethnic background for a moment.

10. Where do you tend to hear or participate in the most conversations about race or racism? How do you typically feel or respond?

11. How important is race, ethnicity, or your immigration story to your sense of who you are?

12. Can you give me an example of why or how race or ethnicity has shaped your life so far?

13. Now turning to gender and sexuality: How do you and your friends talk about gender identity or LGBTQ issues?

    The interviewee may want to clarify terms. First try turning the question back to the participant: What do you think people mean when they use that term? What are other terms you hear? We're less interested in you giving a "right" or "wrong" answer and more interested in how you and your peers discuss these kinds of things, including what's confusing.

14. How frequently do these questions come up?

15. How does this topic usually come up in conversations?

16. How do you think your own sense of gender has shaped the way you think about yourself?

17. What do you think God thinks about some of these concerns related to race, ethnic background, and gender identity? How do you think God would want people to respond to one another in these areas?

18. At your church, do you talk about some of these more than others? Are there any of these issues you *never* hear people talking about at church?

19. How do your own views about some of these issues differ from your church's? Do you talk about those differences with anyone? How does that experience usually go?

Belonging

Now I'm going to ask a similar set of questions about belonging, plus some different ones. The first time we spoke you named these words or phrases as responses to the question "Where do I belong?": (insert words or phrases).

20. I wonder how you feel about those responses now. What do you like about these descriptions? How would you change or add to them?

21. How do you think your answers have changed over time in your life so far?

22. What words or terms would your family want you to use to talk about belonging?

23. How do those words make you feel?

    If the participant has shared about a particularly disruptive childhood event, like immigrating to the US as a child, moving around a lot, or the death of a family member, ask:

24. You've shared about (disruptive childhood event). Has that experience shaped your sense of belonging—making it either easier or harder for you to feel like you belong in other situations?

25. Have you ever done something to impress others you were with? Can you think of an example or story?

26. At your church, do you feel as though you are an important part of the community and belong there?

27. Sometimes people think about belonging in terms of safety—who they feel safe around or where they feel safest. How does that understanding of belonging feel to you?

28. When do you tend to feel most alone?

29. Another aspect of belonging is in dating or romantic relationships. What are some of the expectations or views around dating in your family, your church, and your school, and how are they different?

30. What is your own perspective on dating and romantic relationships?

31. Have you been in a dating relationship?

32. What was that like?

33. What is something you've learned about yourself because of a dating relationship?

Purpose

Now we're going to turn to purpose, or a sense of doing something with our lives that matters in some way to us and to others. The first time we spoke you shared these words or phrases related to questions about purpose: (insert words or phrases).

34. I wonder how you feel about those responses now. What do you like about these descriptions? How would you change or add to them?

35. How do you think your answers have changed over time in your life so far?

36. As you think about other people your age, how would their responses to questions about purpose be similar to yours? How would they be different?

37. How does your family talk about purpose, or how would they want you to talk about your purpose?

38. How, if at all, has your church or faith impacted your sense of purpose?

39. How do you wish your church would better shape, or impact, your sense of purpose?

40. What words or terms do you think leaders at your church would want you to use to describe your sense of purpose? How are these words similar to the words you would use? How are they different?

41. Would you say you've ever had a sense of "calling" or used that word to describe something you want to do? What is that like for you?

42. In what ways do you think the choices you make are shaped by your purpose in life?

43. As you think about finishing high school and moving on to what is next, what are your goals or dreams in life? How do you plan to achieve them?

44. How do you think your faith and church might continue to shape you in the future?

Exploring Youth Concerns, Struggles, and Actions in the World

We'd also like to hear more about your concerns, particularly related to the world we live in. Earlier we talked about issues related to race, culture, and gender. Now think broadly about things that might concern you in the world.

45. Tell me about some of the concerns and struggles, both personal and social, that you or other youth face. What are some things that you or other teenagers talk or worry about?

46. When you look around your school, your community, our country, or the world, what kinds of concerns do you have or what things do you want to see changed? What really stands out to you as problems that need to be addressed?

47. What types of things are you doing now that address any of these concerns?

48. How does your church, faith, or understanding of God help you to think about or make sense of the struggles or concerns that you or other youth have?

49. Do you have specific people you take your questions and struggles to? (Can you talk to a leader in your church, a friend, or others?)

50. Have you ever had a sense of God calling you to work for change or to make a difference in some way? Can you explain or describe this?

Happiness

51. To you, what does it mean to be happy or to have a happy life?

52. Can you think of a time recently when you did something to make someone else happy? Tell me more about that.

53. And what about a time when you did something to lessen someone's unhappiness?

54. How often do you think making someone else happy or less unhappy motivates what you do?

55. Does making other people happy ever become a problem for you? How so?

Concluding Questions

56. What was it like to share about your life like this over the course of these interviews? Was anything surprising, difficult, or helpful to talk about?

57. What else, if anything, do you want us to know about that we may be missing or may not have asked?

Notes

Chapter 1 The Big Questions Every Teenager Is Asking

1. Harvard Medical School, "Data Table 1: Lifetime Prevalence DSM-IV/WMH-CIDI Disorders by Sex and Cohort," "National Comorbidity Survey (NCS)," 2007, https://www.hcp.med.harvard.edu/ncs/index.php; and Borwin Bandelow and Sophie Michaelis, "Epidemiology of Anxiety Disorders in the 21st Century," *Dialogues in Clinical Neuroscience* 17, no. 3 (September 2015): 327–35.

2. M. É. Czeisler et al., "Mental Health, Substance Use, and Suicidal Ideation during the COVID-19 Pandemic—United States, June 24–30, 2020," *Morbidity Mortality Weekly Report* 69, no. 32 (August 14, 2020): 1049–57, http://dx.doi.org/10.15585/mmwr.mm6932a1.

3. Mathilde M. Husky et al., "Twelve-Month Suicidal Symptoms and Use of Services among Adolescents: Results from the National Comorbidity Survey," *Psychiatric Services* 63, no. 12 (October 2012), https://www.ncbi.nlm.nih.gov/pmc/articles/PMC5100004/. The suicide rate among US children and young adults ages ten to twenty-four rose 56 percent between 2007 and 2017. Sally C. Curtin and Melonie Heron, "Death Rates Due to Suicide and Homicide among Persons Aged 10–24: United States, 2000–2017," National Center for Health Statistics Data Brief, no. 352, October 2018, https://www.cdc.gov/nchs/data/databriefs/db352-h.pdf.

4. Forty-five percent. Katherine Schaeffer, "Most U.S. Teens Who Use Cellphones Do It to Pass Time, Connect with Others, Learn New Things," Pew Research Center, August 23, 2019, https://www.pewresearch.org/fact-tank/2019/08/23/most-u-s-teens-who-use-cellphones-do-it-to-pass-time-connect-with-others-learn-new-things/.

5. JingJing Jaing, "How Teens and Parents Navigate Screen Time and Device Distractions," Pew Research Center, August 20, 2018, https://www.pewresearch.org/internet/2018/08/22/how-teens-and-parents-navigate-screen-time-and-device-distractions.

6. Jaing, "How Teens and Parents Navigate Screen Time and Device Distractions."

7. Amanda Lenhart, "Chapter 4: Social Media and Friendships," Pew Research Center, August 4, 2015, https://www.pewresearch.org/internet/2015/08/06/chapter-4-social-media-and-friendships/.

8. Covenant Eyes, Inc., "Porn Stats: 250+ Facts, Quotes, and Statistics about Pornography Use (2018 Edition)," 14–15, file:///C:/Users/mtimm/Downloads/covenant-eyes-porn-stats-2018-edition.pdf.

9. Centers for Disease Control and Prevention, "Youth Risk Behavior Survey: Data Summary and Trends Report 2017," 36, https://www.cdc.gov/healthyyouth/data/yrbs/pdf/trendsreport.pdf.

10. Estimates predict that by 2060, young people under eighteen will be roughly one-third Hispanic, one-third White, and hovering around 10 percent each for African American, Asian American, and multiracial groups. This means the percentage of multiracial young people in particular will double by then. While about two-thirds of all census-counted US Americans are White today, projections estimate that percentage to drop to under 44 percent by 2060. Adapted from Kara Powell and Kat Armas, "America's 2020 Ethnic Reality—And What It Means For You," Fuller Youth Institute, January 16, 2020, https://fulleryouthinstitute.org/blog/americas-2020-ethnic-reality, which is based on data compiled from S. L. Colby and J. M. Ortman, "Projections of the Size and Composition of the US Population: 2014 to 2060: Population Estimates and Projections," 2015, https://www.census.gov/content/dam/Census/library/publications/2015/demo/p25-1143.pdf, and "Quick Facts," US Census Bureau, 2018, https://www.census.gov/quickfacts/fact/table/US/PST045218.

11. Candice L. Odgers and Michael B. Robb, *Tweens, Teens, Tech, and Mental Health* (San Francisco: Common Sense Media, 2020), 17; citing statistics from "Immigrant Children," *Child Trends*, 2018, https://www.childtrends.org/?indicators=immigrant-children.

12. Gary J. Gates, "In U.S., More Adults Identifying as LGBT," Gallup, January 11, 2017, https://news.gallup.com/poll/201731/lgbt-identification-rises.aspx.

13. Gates, "In U.S., More Adults Identifying as LGBT."

14. Jody L Herman et al., "Age of Individuals Who Identify as Transgender in the United States," Williams Institute UCLA School of Law, 2017, 2, https://williamsinstitute.law.ucla.edu/wp-content/uploads/TransAgeReport.pdf; and Michelle M. Johns et al., "Transgender Identity and Experiences of Violence Victimization, Substance Use, Suicide Risk, and

Sexual Risk Behaviors among High School Students—19 States and Large Urban School Districts, 2017," *Morbidity and Mortality Weekly Report* 68, no. 3 (2019): 67–71.

15. Centers for Disease Control and Prevention, "Youth Risk Behavior Survey: Data Summary and Trends Report 2017," 10–11.

16. "Spotlight on School Safety," YouthTruth Student Survey, 2018, https://youthtruthsurvey.org/spotlight-on-school-safety/.

17. Almost two-thirds (64 percent) of teens of color, including 73 percent of Hispanics, say they are at least "somewhat worried" about a school shooting, compared with 51 percent of White teens. Nikki Graf, "A Majority of U.S. Teens Fear a Shooting Could Happen at Their School, and Most Parents Share Their Concern," Pew Research Center, April 18, 2018, https://www.pewresearch.org/fact-tank/2018/04/18/a-majority -of-u-s-teens-fear-a-shooting-could-happen-at-their-school-and-most -parents-share-their-concern/.

18. "Vaping of Marijuana on the Rise among Teens: NIH's 2019 Monitoring the Future Survey Finds Continuing Declines in Prescription Opioid Misuse, Tobacco Cigarettes, and Alcohol," National Institute on Drug Abuse, December 18, 2019, https://www.drugabuse.gov/news -events/news-releases/2019/12/vaping-marijuana-rise-among-teens.

19. University of Michigan Institute for Social Research, "National Adolescent Drug Trends in 2019: Findings Released," December 18, 2019, http://www.monitoringthefuture.org/pressreleases/19drugpr.pdf.

20. "Vaping of Marijuana on the Rise among Teens."

21. Our estimate that 40 to 50 percent of high school graduates will fail to stick with their faith is based on a compilation of data from the following various studies. A 2011 study of young adults indicates that approximately 59 percent of young people with a Christian background report that they have dropped out of church. David Kinnaman and Aly Hawkins, *You Lost Me* (Grand Rapids: Baker Books, 2011), 23. According to a Gallup poll, approximately 40 percent of eighteen- to twenty-nine-year-olds who attended church when they were sixteen or seventeen years old are no longer attending. George H. Gallup Jr., "The Religiosity Cycle," Gallup, June 4, 2002, https://news.gallup.com/poll/6124/religiosity -cycle.aspx; and Frank Newport, "A Look at Religious Switching in America Today," Gallup, June 23, 2006, https://news.gallup.com/poll/23467 /look-religious-switching-america-today.aspx. A 2007 survey by LifeWay Research of over one thousand adults ages eighteen to thirty who spent a year or more in youth group during high school suggests that more than 65 percent of young adults who attend a Protestant church for at least a year in high school will stop attending church regularly for at least a year between the ages of eighteen and twenty-two. In this study, respondents were not necessarily seniors who had graduated from youth group. In

addition, the research design did not factor in parachurch or on-campus faith communities in their definition of college "church" attendance. Data from the National Study of Youth and Religion indicates that 20 to 35 percent of Roman Catholic and Protestant teenagers who were religious become young adults who are no longer religious. Christian Smith with Patricia Snell, *Souls in Transition: The Religious & Spiritual Lives of Emerging Adults* (New York: Oxford University Press, 2009), 109–10. In a Pew study of faith transition for US adults in general, roughly half of the US population changed religion at some point in their lives. "Faith in Flux," Pew Research Center, February 2011, http://www.pewforum .org/2009/04/27/faith-in-flux/. In a more recent compilation of research, forty-two million young people are expected to leave the Christian church (across Roman Catholic, mainline, and evangelical traditions) between 2020 and 2050. "The Great Opportunity," Pinetops Foundation, 2018, www.greatopportunity.org.

22. "In US, Decline of Christianity Continues at Rapid Pace," Pew Research Center, October 17, 2019, https://www.pewforum.org/2019/10 /17/in-u-s-decline-of-christianity-continues-at-rapid-pace/. Generational theorists Neil Howe and William Strauss are credited with designating millennials as those generally born between 1980 and 2000. Other birth-year designations for millennials have been developed, but they tend to overlap heavily with the birth years of 1980–2000. See Neil Howe and William Strauss, *Millennials Rising: The Next Great Generation* (New York: Vintage, 2000).

23. Martin B. Copenhaver, *Jesus Is the Question: The 307 Questions Jesus Asked and the 3 He Answered* (Nashville: Abingdon, 2014), xviii.

24. First shared in Kara E. Powell, Brad M. Griffin, and Cheryl A. Crawford, *Sticky Faith Youth Worker Edition* (Grand Rapids: Zondervan, 2011), 143–44.

Chapter 2 Learning to Listen for Answers

1. Generally, young people from racial and ethnic minority groups are less likely to receive mental health care than White adolescents, and boys are less likely to get help than girls. Further, there is evidence that mental health stigma tends to be higher among young people of color. See Janet R. Cummings and Benjamin G. Druss, "Racial/Ethnic Differences in Mental Health Service Use among Adolescents with Major Depression," *Journal of the American Academy of Child and Adolescent Psychiatry* 50, no. 2 (2011): 160–70; and M. J. DuPont-Reyes, A. P. Villatoro, J. C. Phelan, K. Painter, and B. G. Link, "Adolescent Views of Mental Illness Stigma: An Intersectional Lens," *American Journal of Orthopsychiatry* 90, no. 2 (2020): 201–11.

2. By "intersectionality," we mean the interconnected nature of social categories such as race, class, and gender that can be experienced by an individual or group. The term was originally coined by Black feminist scholar Kimberlé Williams Crenshaw, cofounder of the African American Policy Forum, and has come to be used widely across many disciplines, including practical theology.

3. Narrative analysis "focuses on stories" and "examines human lives through the lens of a narrative, honoring lived experience as a source of important knowledge and understanding." Michael Quinn Patton, *Qualitative Research & Evaluation Methods: Integrating Theory and Practice*, 4th ed. (Thousand Oaks, CA: SAGE Publications, 2014), 128. Narrative analysis is typically considered a flexible approach that employs various methodologies and analytic strategies. See D. Jean Clandinin and F. Michael Connelly, *Narrative Inquiry: Experience and Story in Qualitative Research* (San Francisco: Jossey-Bass, 2004), 154; and Sharan B. Merriam, *Qualitative Research: A Guide to Design and Implementation*, 3rd ed. (San Francisco: Jossey-Bass, 2009), 32–34, 202–3. We also drew from Nancy Tatom Ammerman, *Sacred Stories, Spiritual Tribes: Finding Religion in Everyday Life* (New York: Oxford University Press, 2013); Jenny Pak, *Korean American Women: Stories of Acculturation and Changing Selves* (New York: Routledge, 2012); Dan P. McAdams and Erika Manczak, "Personality and the Life Story," in *APA Handbook of Personality and Social Psychology*, vol. 4, *Personality Processes and Individual Differences*, ed. Mario Mikulincer and Phillip R. Shaver (Washington, DC: American Psychological Association, 2015), 425–46, https://doi.org/10.1037/14343-019; Christian Smith and Melinda Lundquist Denton, "Methodological Design and Procedures for the National Survey of Youth and Religion (NSYR) Personal Interviews," University of North Carolina at Chapel Hill, 2003, https://youthandreligion.nd.edu /assets/102495/personalivmethods.pdf; and Almeda Wright, *The Spiritual Lives of Young African Americans* (New York: Oxford University Press, 2017).

4. Our racial/ethnic backgrounds include African American (1), Latina (2), Asian American (3), and White (4). Interviews were conducted from summer 2019 to summer 2020.

5. Specific state representation included eighteen from California (Los Angeles and five other cities in LA/Orange County); two from Michigan (Grand Rapids area and rural); four from North Carolina (four communities across the state); one from Texas (Dallas area); and two from Maryland (suburban DC area). Our sample skewed toward later high school in order to hear from young people who were developmentally more able to reflect on their experiences and the 3 big questions.

6. We are especially grateful to Gabriella Silva for conducting various coding analyses with transcript data and to our project expert advisors, who included Steven Argue, Scott Cormode, Joi Freeman, Jenny Pak, Montague Williams, and Almeda Wright. Jake Mulder provided overall Living a Better Story (LABS) project leadership and additional protocol construction input.

7. Twelve focus groups were conducted with thirty-five teenagers to solicit input and clarification on narrative wording. Groups took place in California, North Carolina, and Michigan. Among these participants, the racial/ethnic makeup included fifteen White, seven Latino/a, eight Asian American (Chinese, Filipina, Indonesian, Japanese, and Korean), and three African American.

8. The literature review team was led by Aaron Yenney and included Kat Armas, Roslyn Hernández, Helen Jun, Quanesha Moore, Gabriella Silva, and Sam Zheng Ning.

9. The Sticky Faith Innovation project was funded by Lilly Endowment, Inc. and explored the development of a cohort-based ministry innovation process with churches from across the country. Insights from the project are peppered throughout the book, thanks to the work of the project team led by Steve Argue and managed by Caleb Roose. Steve and Caleb wrote about this process in *Sticky Faith Innovation* (see fuller youthinstitute.org for details and to purchase copies). Tyler Greenway performed linguistic inquiry and word count analyses on responses from the 2,092 participants—insights that appear periodically alongside our interview analyses.

10. For the sake of confidentiality, all participant names have been changed and at times other details have been altered in stories. While we stick as close as possible to original language, we have edited participant quotes for readability and occasionally have combined statements to smooth them out (we're sparing you a lot of "likes" and "ums"). We believe what you are reading remains true to the thoughts and perspectives shared in interviews and focus groups.

11. Dietrich Bonhoeffer, *Life Together*, trans. John W. Doberstein, rev. ed. (1949; repr., New York: HarperCollins, 1954), 97–98.

12. Kara Powell, Jake Mulder, and Brad M. Griffin, *Growing Young: Six Essential Strategies to Help Young People Discover and Love Your Church* (Grand Rapids: Baker Books, 2016), 91–92.

13. This definition and the following insights are derived largely from M. H. Davis, *Empathy: A Social Psychological Approach* (New York: Routledge, 1994).

14. These research insights from the Sticky Faith Innovation project were originally published by our FYI colleagues Steven C. Argue and Tyler S. Greenway. See their "Empathy with Emerging Generations as a

Foundation for Ministry," *Christian Education Journal* 17, no. 1 (2020): 110–29.

15. Adapted from former Fuller Seminary professor David W. Augsburger, *Caring Enough to Hear and Be Heard* (Ventura, CA: Regal Books, 1982), 12.

Chapter 3 Jesus Offers Better Answers

1. We've chosen to use the term *discipleship* most commonly in this book, but depending on your tradition, you might be more comfortable with terms such as *formation* or *spiritual formation*.

2. "Trust" was included with belief when its usage was oriented more toward belief language than relationship.

3. For example, Matthew 4:19; Mark 1:17; Luke 5:27; John 1:43.

4. Our yes to God is a response to God's yes to humanity through Jesus Christ (2 Cor. 1:19–20). Also see E. Stanley Jones, *The Divine Yes* (Nashville: Abingdon, 1975), 13, 15, 22. According to theologian Karl Barth, God's "first and last word is Yes and not No." Karl Barth, *Church Dogmatics*, vol. 2, part 2, ed. G. W. Bromiley and T. F. Torrance (Edinburgh: T&T Clark, 1957).

5. "Not that I have already obtained all this, or have already arrived at my goal, but I press on to take hold of that for which Christ Jesus took hold of me" (Phil. 3:12; cf. Phil. 2:12; Rom. 12:1–2).

6. N. T. Wright suggests that character is the "What now?" for Christians. Or our teenagers might wonder, *What today? How does my faith relate to today—what's in front of me today?* See N. T. Wright, *After You Believe: Why Christian Character Matters* (San Francisco: HarperOne, 2012).

7. Matthew 22:37–40; Mark 12:29–31; Luke 10:25–37.

8. Micah 6:8.

9. Luke 14:27; cf. Mark 8:34–35.

10. See Dietrich Bonhoeffer, *The Cost of Discipleship*, trans. Reginald H. Fuller (New York: Macmillan, 1959). Note that in communities of color, the theme of suffering for God can become another means of oppression. Jacquelyn Grant argues against "the sin of servanthood" for African Americans, given the historical baggage and contemporary realities "servant" carries for people (particularly women) of color. See Jacquelyn Grant, "The Sin of Servanthood and the Deliverance of Discipleship," in *Troubling in My Soul: Womanist Perspectives on Evil and Suffering*, ed. Emilie Townes (Maryknoll, NY: Orbis Books, 1993).

11. This framework roughly follows an adapted practical theology method first introduced in Chap Clark and Kara Powell, *Deep Ministry in a Shallow World: Not-So-Secret Findings about Youth Ministry* (Grand Rapids: Zondervan, 2006).

Chapter 4 The Big Question of Identity

1. Steven Levenson, Benji Pasek, and Justin Paul, *Dear Evan Hanson* (New York: Theatre Communications Group, 2017), 8.

2. Kelby Clark, "How Gen Z Is Changing the Face of Modern Beauty," ViacomCBS, March 7, 2019, https://www.viacom.com/news/how-gen -z-is-changing-the-face-of-modern-beauty.

3. For the most part, the current answers we enumerate in this chapter, as well as in chapters 6 and 8, emerge from a blend of our literature review and our interviews. On those rare occasions when the findings from previous research and our interviews didn't align, it's fair to say we preferenced our interviews (because they offered face-to-face interaction with diverse teenagers today).

4. Andrew Root, *The End of Youth Ministry? Why Parents Don't Really Care about Youth Groups and What Youth Workers Should Do about It* (Grand Rapids: Baker Academic, 2020), 183.

5. Claudia is describing "code switching," or the (often demanding) practice of alternating between different languages or different manners of speech based on your audience.

6. Alice E. Marwick, *Status Update: Celebrity, Publicity, and Branding in the Social Media Age* (New Haven: Yale University Press, 2013), 191–94.

7. Sarah Weise, *InstaBrain: The New Rules for Marketing to Generation Z* (Independently Published, 2019), 39.

8. Malcolm Harris, *Kids These Days: Human Capital and the Making of Millennials* (New York: Little, Brown, 2017), 3–12.

9. Joi Freeman, conversation with the author (Brad Griffin), July 16, 2020. Find more of Joi's work on Gen Z at remnantstrategy.com.

10. Jennifer D. Rubin and Sara I. McClelland, "'Even Though It's a Small Checkbox, It's a Big Deal': Stresses and Strains of Managing Sexual Identity(s) on Facebook," *Culture, Health & Sexuality* 17, no. 4 (January 14, 2015): 512–26.

Chapter 5 ENOUGH: Jesus' Better Answer

1. Dante (not his real name) was part of a focus group, and therefore his profile does not appear in appendix A with interview participants.

2. Marianne Meye-Thompson, *John: A Commentary*, New Testament Library Series (Louisville: Westminster John Knox, 2015), 141.

3. Early church father Chrystostom argues that Andrew's response doesn't trust that Jesus can work with such skimpy offerings. *Saint Chrysostom: Homilies on the Gospel of St. John and the Epistles to the Hebrews: Nicene and Post-Nicene Fathers of the Christian Church*, part 14, ed. Philip Schaff (Whitefish, MT: Kessinger Publishing, 2004), 150.

4. John 6:10 indicates that there were about five thousand men gathered; factoring in women and children (always a good idea!), the overall crowd size was likely somewhere between ten to fifteen thousand. Craig S. Keener, *The IVP Bible Background Commentary: New Testament* (Downers Grove, IL: InterVarsity, 2014), 265.

5. Marva J. Dawn, *In the Beginning, GOD: Creation, Culture, and the Spiritual Life* (Downers Grove, IL: InterVarsity, 2009), 44.

6. The Greek word is παιδάριον (or *paidarion*, pronounced "pah-ee-DAR-ee-on"), which is neuter, meaning it's a non-gendered noun.

7. Devin English, Sharon F. Lambert, Brendesha M. Tynes, Lisa Bowleg et al., "Daily Multidimensional Racial Discrimination among Black U.S. American Adolescents," *Journal of Applied Developmental Psychology* 66 (January–February 2020): 8.

8. Brenda Salter McNeil and Rick Richardson, *The Heart of Racial Justice* (Downers Grove, IL: InterVarsity, 2004), 88.

9. Walter Brueggemann, *Sabbath as Resistance: Saying No to the Culture of Now* (Louisville: Westminster John Knox, 2014), 6.

10. These disciplines are illustrative and are by no means comprehensive.

11. Nathan T. Stucky, *Wrestling with Rest* (Grand Rapids: Eerdmans, 2020), 7.

12. Eugene H. Peterson, *Working the Angles: The Shape of Pastoral Integrity* (Grand Rapids: Eerdmans, 1987), 52.

Chapter 6 The Big Question of Belonging

1. David Arnold, *The Strange Fascinations of Noah Hypnotik* (New York: Viking, 2018), 394.

2. Douglas Nemecek, "Cigna U.S. Loneliness Index," Cigna, May 2018, https://www.multivu.com/players/English/8294451-cigna-us-lone liness-survey/docs/IndexReport_1524069371598-173525450.pdf. According to this study, loneliness has reached "epidemic levels."

3. Julianne Holt-Lunstad et al., "Loneliness and Social Isolation as Risk Factors for Mortality: A Meta-Analytic Review," *Perspectives on Psychological Science* 10, no. 2 (March 1, 2015): 227–37.

4. Eric Klinenberg, "Is Loneliness a Health Epidemic?," *New York Times*, February 9, 2018, https://www.nytimes.com/2018/02/09/opinion /sunday/loneliness-health.html.

5. Claudia Hammond, "The Surprising Truth about Loneliness," *BBC*, September 30, 2018, https://www.bbc.com/future/article/20180928-the -surprising-truth-about-loneliness. Hammond reports on a 2018 survey of fifty-five thousand people from around the world.

6. Nemecek, "Cigna U.S. Loneliness Index."

7. D. Anderson-Butcher and D. E. Conroy, "Factorial and Criterion Validity of Scores of a Measure of Belonging in Youth Development Programs," *Educational and Psychological Measurement* 62, no. 5 (2002): 857–76.

8. Benjamin Hanckel and Alan Morris, "Finding Community and Contesting Heteronormativity: Queer Young People's Engagement in an Australian Online Community," *Journal of Youth Studies* 17, no. 7 (August 2014): 872–86; and Yvette Taylor, Emily Falconer, and Ria Snowdon, "Queer Youth, Facebook and Faith: Facebook Methodologies and Online Identities," *New Media & Society* 16, no. 7 (November 1, 2014): 1138–53.

9. Bonnie Hagerty et al., "Sense of Belonging: A Vital Mental Health Concept," *Archives of Psychiatric Nursing* 6, no. 3 (1992): 172–77; and Bonnie Hagerty et al., "An Emerging Theory of Human Relatedness," *Image: The Journal of Nursing Scholarship* 25, no. 4 (1993): 291–96.

Chapter 7 WITH: Jesus' Better Answer

1. Brené Brown, *Braving the Wilderness: The Quest for True Belonging and the Courage to Stand Alone* (New York: Penguin Random House, 2017), 158.

2. Tommy Givens, "Reimagining the Gospel in Relationship: What Does the Gospel Mean for Teenagers and Friendship?," Fuller Youth Institute, January 4, 2014, https://fulleryouthinstitute.org/articles/reimagining -the-gospel-in-relationship-part-1.

3. Andrew Root writes, "In the life of a disciple, friendship is a hyper-good. . . . It's what we're created for, to be God's friend." Andrew Root, *The End of Youth Ministry? Why Parents Don't Really Care about Youth Groups and What Youth Workers Should Do about It* (Grand Rapids: Baker Academic, 2020), 224.

4. Christine Pohl, *Living into Community: Cultivating Practices That Sustain Us* (Grand Rapids: Eerdmans, 2011), 2.

5. Willie James Jennings, *Acts*, Belief: A Theological Commentary on the Bible (Louisville: Westminster John Knox, 2017), 8.

6. Carl McColman, *The Big Book of Christian Mysticism: The Essential Guide to Contemplative Spirituality* (Charlottesville, VA: Hampton Roads Publishing, 2010), 165–66.

7. See Dietrich Bonhoeffer, *Life Together*, trans. John W. Doberstein, rev. ed. (1949; repr., New York: HarperCollins, 1954), 35, 116.

8. Gerhard Lohfink calls this a "contrast-society," in Gerhard Lohfink, *Jesus and Community: The Social Dimension of Christian Faith*, trans. John P. Calvin (Philadelphia: Fortress, 1982), 56, 62.

9. For an incredibly helpful article about the ways this can play out in multiethnic youth ministries, see Trey Clark, "Unity Does Not Equal

Uniformity: Lessons Learned in Multiethnic Youth Ministry," Fuller Youth Institute, October 6, 2017, https://fulleryouthinstitute.org/articles /unity-uniformity. Also see Christena Cleveland, *Disunity in Christ: Uncovering the Hidden Forces That Keep Us Apart* (Downers Grove, IL: InterVarsity, 2013).

10. Kathy Khang, *Raise Your Voice: Why We Stay Silent and How to Speak Up* (Downers Grove, IL: InterVarsity, 2018), 41.

11. Mitzi J. Smith and Yung Suk Kim, *Toward Decentering the New Testament: A Reintroduction* (Eugene, OR: Cascade Books, 2018).

12. Gregory Boyle, *Barking at the Choir: The Power of Radical Kinship* (New York: Simon & Schuster, 2017), 3.

13. Mother Teresa, *Where There Is Love, There Is God: Her Path to Closer Union with God and Greater Love for Others*, ed. Brian Kolodiekchuk (New York: Image, 2012), 330.

14. Smith and Kim, *Toward Decentering the New Testament*, 177.

15. Pohl, *Living into Community*, 4.

16. Scott Cormode developed the background content for this section on hospitality as part of FYI's Sticky Faith Innovation project.

17. Miroslav Volf, *Exclusion and Embrace: A Theological Exploration of Identity, Otherness, and Reconciliation* (Nashville: Abingdon, 1996), 129.

18. In our Growing Young research, we uncovered the practice of "keychain leadership," equipping young people with significant responsibility and access to influence within their church. See Kara Powell, Jake Mulder, and Brad M. Griffin, *Growing Young: Six Essential Strategies to Help Young People Discover and Love Your Church* (Grand Rapids: Baker Books, 2016).

Chapter 8 The Big Question of Purpose

1. "Like a compass that always points north, a purpose in life consistently orients and motivates an individual toward a personally significant aim." Kendall Cotton Bronk, *Purpose in Life: A Critical Component of Optimal Youth Development* (Dordrecht, Netherlands: Springer Science & Business Media, 2014), 6. The positive effects of purpose for teenagers and young adults include lower risk of self-destructive behavior and a markedly positive attitude that generates an eagerness to learn about the world. William Damon, *The Path to Purpose: Helping Our Children Find Their Calling in Life* (New York: Simon & Schuster, 2008), 31.

2. Emily Esfahani Smith, *The Power of Meaning: Crafting a Life That Matters* (New York: Penguin Random House, 2017), 24.

3. See William Damon, *Noble Purpose: The Joy of Living a Meaningful Life* (West Conshohocken, PA: Templeton Foundation Press, 2003).

4. Bronk, *Purpose in Life*, 7.

5. Roberta Katz, "How Gen Z Is Different, According to Social Scientists," *Pacific Standard*, April 2, 2019, https://psmag.com/ideas/how-gen -z-is-different-according-to-social-scientists.

6. Martin E. P. Seligman et al., "Positive Education: Positive Psychology and Classroom Interventions," *Oxford Review of Education* 35, no. 3 (2009): 301.

7. This definition of *agency* is adapted from Kara Powell and Steven Argue, *Growing With: Every Parent's Guide to Helping Teenagers and Young Adults Thrive in Their Faith, Family, and Future* (Grand Rapids: Baker Books, 2019), 136.

8. Corey Seemiller and Meghan Grace, *Generation Z: A Century in the Making* (New York: Routledge, 2018), 32–33.

9. Sophia Pink, "I Drove across America to Find Out What Makes Gen Z Tick," *Pacific Standard*, April 8, 2019, https://psmag.com/ideas /road-tripping-to-understand-gen-z.

Chapter 9 STORY: Jesus' Better Answer

1. Kevin J. Vanhoozer, *Faith Speaking Understanding: Performing the Drama of Doctrine* (Louisville: Westminster John Knox, 2014), 59.

2. Dan P. McAdams, *The Art and Science of Personality Development* (New York: Guilford Press, 2015), 240, emphasis original.

3. Alasdair MacIntyre, *After Virtue* (Notre Dame, IN: University of Notre Dame Press, 1981), 216.

4. Eugene H. Peterson, *Eat This Book: A Conversation in the Art of Spiritual Reading* (Grand Rapids: Eerdmans, 2009), 44.

5. The most observant Jewish believers followed Paul. Those more intellectually sophisticated rallied around Apollos, a Hellenized Jew who likely helped found the church in Ephesus with his mentors, Priscilla and Aquilla. Michael J. Gorman, *Apostle of the Crucified Lord: A Theological Introduction to Paul & His Letters*, 2nd ed. (Grand Rapids: Eerdmans, 2017), 234; and L. M. McDonald, "Ephesus," in *Dictionary of New Testament Background: A Compendium of Contemporary Biblical Scholarship*, ed. Craig A. Evans and Stanley E. Porter Jr. (Downers Grove, IL: InterVarsity, 2010), 319.

6. Craig G. Bartholomew and Michael W. Goheen, *The Drama of Scripture: Finding Our Place in the Biblical Story* (Grand Rapids: Baker Academic, 2014), 22–23; and N. T. Wright, "How Can the Bible Be Authoritative?," *Vox Evangelica* 21 (1991): 7–32, https://ntwrightpage.com /2016/07/12/how-can-the-bible-be-authoritative/.

7. There are more or less complex versions of this, including the simplest of creation, fall, new creation. We've also really appreciated Michael

Novelli's *Shaped by the Story: Helping Students Encounter God in a New Way* (Grand Rapids: Zondervan, 2008).

8. Samuel Wells, *Improvisation: The Drama of Christian Ethics* (Grand Rapids: Brazos, 2004), 65.

9. The "Life Story Interview" approach was developed primarily by Dan P. McAdams and has been widely used, critiqued, and amended. See Dan P. McAdams and Kate C. McLean, "Narrative Identity," *Current Directions in Psychological Science* 22, no. 3 (2013): 233–38, https://doi.org/10.1177/0963721413475622. See also Daniel Taylor, *Tell Me a Story: The Life-Shaping Power of Our Stories* (St. Paul: Bog Walk Press, 2001), 165.

10. *Shalom* (pronounced "shah-LOME") is a Hebrew word in the Old Testament often translated "peace" but intended to mean holistic flourishing. "Evidently justice has something to do with the fact that God's love for each and every one of God's human creatures takes the form of God desiring the shalom of each and every one." Nicholas Wolterstorff, "The Contours of Justice: An Ancient Call for Shalom," in *God and the Victim: Theological Reflections on Evil, Victimization, Justice, and Forgiveness*, ed. Lisa Barnes Lampman and Michelle D. Shattuck (Grand Rapids: Eerdmans, 1999), 113.

11. We are grateful for Jeremy Del Rio for this helpful definition of *justice*, which we used in Chap Clark and Kara E. Powell, *Deep Justice in a Broken World* (Grand Rapids: Zondervan, 2007), 10.

12. Martin Luther King Jr., "Beyond Vietnam: A Time to Break Silence" (speech, New York, NY, April 4, 1967).

13. Frederick Buechner, *Wishful Thinking: A Seeker's ABC* (San Francisco: HarperOne, 1993), 118–19.

14. Kurt Ver Beek, "The Impact of Short-Term Missions: A Case Study of House Construction in Honduras after Hurricane Mitch," *Missiology* 34, no. 4 (October 2006): 485.

15. A major thanks to David Livermore, leader of the Cultural Intelligence Center, and Terry Linhart of Bethel College (Indiana) for collaborating with us in developing this model. See Kara Powell and Brad M. Griffin, *Sticky Faith Service Guide* (Grand Rapids: Zondervan, 2016), 19.

16. P. A. Fry, "The Development of Personal Meaning and Wisdom in Adolescence: A Reexamination of Moderating and Consolidating Factors and Influences," in *The Human Quest for Meaning: A Handbook of Psychological Research and Clinical Applications*, 2nd ed., ed. P. T. P. Wong (New York: Routledge, 1998), 91–110 as referenced in Kendall Cotton Bronk, *Purpose in Life: A Critical Component of Optimal Youth Development* (Dordrecht, Netherlands: Springer Science & Business Media, 2014), 95.

17. MacIntyre, *After Virtue*, 216.

18. Peterson, *Eat This Book*, 44.

19. Buechner, *Wishful Thinking*, 118–19.

Chapter 10 Conversations and Connections in Tough Times

1. Margaret Renkl, "These Kids Are Done Waiting for Change," *New York Times*, June 15, 2020, https://www.nytimes.com/2020/06/15/opinion/nashville-teens-protests.html.

2. Our thinking about this has been shaped by scholars who study resilience in young people, in particular the work of our Fuller colleagues Pamela Ebstyne King and Lisseth Rojas-Flores with the Thrive Center for Human Development. See more about their and others' work at the thrivecenter.org.

3. One longitudinal study found that high school seniors who were able to create meaning through processing difficult high school turning points showed higher levels of psychological well-being than those students who failed to construct meaning, even when controlling for well-being scores obtained three years earlier at the start of high school. Royette Tavernier and Teena Willoughby, "Adolescent Turning Points: The Association Between Meaning-Making and Psychological Well-Being," *Developmental Psychology* 48, no. 4 (2012): 1058–68, https://doi.apa.org/doiLanding?doi=10.1037%2Fa0026326.

4. You might, of course, have an answer to the question. But even if you do, it might be wise to step back and probe a bit before unleashing your "right" answer. Feeling heard may be more important than the answer itself, at least at the moment.

5. This quote and the content for this section were drawn from Kara Powell, "Processing the Tragedy of School Shootings," Fuller Youth Institute, February 15, 2018, https://fulleryouthinstitute.org/blog/processing-the-tragedy-of-school-shootings. For additional resources, see the Child Mind Institute's resources for trauma and grief, https://childmind.org/topics/concerns/trauma-and-grief/, and the Institute for Collective Trauma and Growth, https://www.ictg.org/, in particular their section on faith-based resources.

6. Some portions of this section are adapted from material written by Scott Cormode for the Sticky Faith Innovation project.

7. Walter Brueggemann describes the rhythms of the psalms as moving from *orientation* to *disorientation* to *reorientation*. Sometimes laments include all three; other times they start and end in disorientation. See Walter Brueggemann, *The Psalms and the Life of Faith* (Minneapolis: Fortress, 1995); and Walter Brueggemann, *Spirituality of the Psalms* (Minneapolis: Augsburg Fortress, 2002).

8. One caveat here: pay attention to any lyrics that seem to glorify death or suggest suicidal thinking, especially as an escape from pain. You may want to address this with the student and, if you have concerns about a student's safety, contact a parent or guardian.

9. Justice advocate Lisa Sharon Harper writes, "Shalom is the stuff of the Kingdom. It's what the Kingdom of God looks like in context. . . . To live in God's kingdom, in the way of shalom, requires that we discard our thin understanding of the gospel." Lisa Sharon Harper, *The Very Good Gospel: How Everything Wrong Can Be Made Right* (Colorado Springs: WaterBrook, 2016), 13–14.

Appendix A Our Interview Participants

1. Asian American participant culture of origin (varying from first- to fourth-generation family immigration background) included Chinese, Filipino, Japanese, and Korean. One African American student also indicated part Caribbean family heritage. Arab American is included as a preferred group term, though it does not currently exist as a US Census category. White is used as a broad category for participants of European descent. Race/ethnicity was self-reported, and some young people knew more about their ancestral heritage than others.

2. Socioeconomic status was self-disclosed based on the following scale: How is your family doing financially? Responses included: we have more than enough money; we have enough money; we are struggling to make it from month to month; I'm not sure. We translated these roughly as upper middle, middle, lower, and unsure.

Appendix B Over 170 Questions to Ask a Teenager

1. Our question protocols drew from work by Nancy Ammerman, Jenny Pak, Dan McAdams and Erika Manczak, Christian Smith and Melinda Lundquist Denton, and Almeda Wright. Jenny Pak and Almeda Wright consulted directly on protocol development. Early protocols were piloted with local teenagers for question clarity and length, and our team completed the full interview cycle with four pilot participants before finalizing the protocols. Research and question lists we adapted from include the following: Nancy Tatom Ammerman, *Sacred Stories, Spiritual Tribes: Finding Religion in Everyday Life* (New York: Oxford University Press, 2013); Jenny Pak, *Korean American Women: Stories of Acculturation and Changing Selves* (New York: Routledge, 2012); Dan P. McAdams and Erika Manczak, "Personality and the Life Story," in *APA Handbook of Personality and Social Psychology*, vol. 4, *Personality Processes and Individual Differences*, ed. Mario Mikulincer and

Phillip R. Shaver (Washington, DC: American Psychological Association, 2015), 425–46, https://doi.org/10.1037/14343-019; Christian Smith and Melinda Lundquist Denton, "Methodological Design and Procedures for the National Survey of Youth and Religion (NSYR) Personal Interviews," University of North Carolina at Chapel Hill, 2003, https://youthandreligion.nd.edu/assets/102495/personalivmethods.pdf; and Almeda Wright, *The Spiritual Lives of Young African Americans* (New York: Oxford University Press, 2017).

Kara Powell, PhD, is the chief of leadership formation and executive director of the Fuller Youth Institute (FYI) at Fuller Theological Seminary (see fulleryouthinstitute.org). Named by *Christianity Today* as one of "50 Women to Watch," Kara serves as a youth and family strategist for Orange and speaks regularly at parenting and leadership conferences. Kara has authored or coauthored numerous books, including *Faith in an Anxious World, Growing With, Growing Young, The Sticky Faith Guide for Your Family* and the entire Sticky Faith series, and the series Can I Ask That? 8 Hard Questions about God and Faith. Kara and her husband, Dave, are regularly inspired by the learning and laughter that comes from their three teenage and young adult children.

Web: karapowell.com | Twitter and Instagram: @kpowellfyi | Facebook: Kara.Powell.Author

Brad M. Griffin is the senior director of content for the Fuller Youth Institute, where he develops research-based training for youth workers and parents. A speaker, writer, and volunteer youth pastor, Brad is the coauthor of over a dozen books, including *Faith in an Anxious World, Growing Young,* several Sticky Faith books, *Every Parent's Guide to Navigating Our Digital World,* and the series Can I Ask That? 8 Hard Questions about God and Faith. Brad and his wife, Missy, live in Southern California and share life with their three teenage and young adult children. He also serves as pastor of youth and family ministries at Mountainside Communion.

Web: fulleryouthinstitute.org | Twitter: @bgriffinfyi | Facebook: brad.griffin

Growing up doesn't mean growing apart.
IT MEANS GROWING WITH.

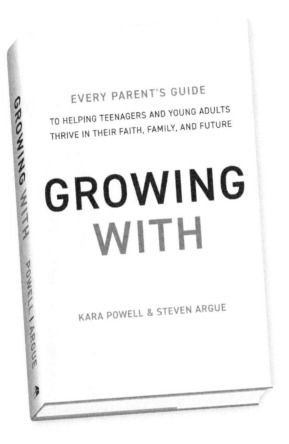

EVERY PARENT'S GUIDE
TO HELPING TEENAGERS AND YOUNG ADULTS
THRIVE IN THEIR FAITH, FAMILY, AND FUTURE

GROWING
WITH

KARA POWELL & STEVEN ARGUE

"As a dad of two teenagers, I couldn't wait for this book!
The mix of real research and real families makes it a valuable
addition to any parent's toolbox."

—JON ACUFF, *New York Times* bestselling author of *Finish*

Your church doesn't need

- ✓ a precise size
- ✓ a trendy location
- ✓ an off-the-charts cool quotient

to make your teenager and young adult love to be there.

6 ESSENTIAL STRATEGIES
TO HELP YOUNG PEOPLE DISCOVER AND LOVE YOUR CHURCH

GROWING YOUNG

KARA POWELL, JAKE MULDER, BRAD GRIFFIN

Find out how remarkable congregations are Growing Young.

fulleryouthinstitute.org/growingyoung

DR. KARA POWELL

Finding answers to leaders' and parents' toughest questions about young people.

Follow Kara to receive blog posts, find out about upcoming resources, and join the conversation at:

karapowell.com

BRAD M. GRIFFIN

Championing teenagers and the
adults who care about them.

Learn about Brad's research-based ministry writing and training at fulleryouthinstitute.org or connect with him on social media!

f @brad.griffin 🐦 @bgriffinfyi

YOUTH LEADERS

Discover research-based resources to
grow lasting faith in young people.

PARENTS

Find practical tools and tips from
faith-filled parents like you.

CHURCH LEADERS

Help your whole church invest
in young people.

 Fuller Youth Institute

Explore our books, curriculum, resources, and more at

FULLERYOUTHINSTITUTE.ORG